CONTENTS

PREFACE

"The whole art of teaching is only the art of awakening the
natural curiosity of young minds."
— Jacques Anatole François Thibault (1881)

Although I cannot speak for the general student population, I do recall my first
animal behavior class being quite a shock. I was not aware that mathematics and
game theory, neurobiology, and endocrinology played such an integral part in the
field. I was enthralled and overwhelmed by the integrative nature of animal behavior in the early 1990s. Today, research in animal behavior and behavioral ecology has progressed in many significant ways, some unimaginable just fifteen years
ago. The field of animal behavior has become more integrative and sophisticated,
and the stacks of articles reporting clever experimental designs, innovative theory,
or noteworthy results climbs closer to the ceiling seemingly every day. From a student's perspective, the advances in animal behavior translate into a vast amount
of introductory material that needs to be covered in a relatively short period of
time. In developing the manual for Dr. Lee Alan Dugatkin's *Principles of Animal
Behavior*, I spent much of my time thinking about ways to alleviate the initial
"shock" of what is covered in a course on animal behavior. I eventually came up
with what I hope is an effective recipe for reviewing the concepts covered in the
text and discussion questions of *Principles of Animal Behavior*.

This manual was created with the interests of both students and instructors in
mind and with the intent of facilitating enjoyable and stimulating student-stu-
dent and student-teacher interactions. Each chapter of the manual begins with
detailed answers to the discussion questions posed at the finale of the corresponding chapter in *Principles of Animal Behavior*. As should be clearly evident
from the first page of the manual, the answers to these questions are directed at
the future intellects of animal behavior rather than established animal behavior-
ists in hopes of *awakening the natural curiosity of young minds*. Dr. Dugatkin

challenges students to color outside the lines in the sense that his questions are geared toward familiarizing students with topics and/or studies that were not, on the whole, covered in great detail in the text. Thus, the answers provided in this manual do not simply revisit the *Principles of Animal Behavior* text verbatim. Rather, I hope that the answers will serve as templates (or even targets) for within-class and extramural discussion sessions, group projects, or lively debates. Furthermore, the discussion questions provided in *Principles of Animal Behavior* would certainly be useful as mock essay exams for students, and the answers I have provided may help to get students' ethological gears turning. Another potential use for this manual would be as a supplemental, in-classroom resource for the students, particularly given that the answers are tailored toward individuals who might be having some trouble wrapping their minds around certain concepts. Lastly, I hope that the answers to the discussion questions provide a useful resource for instructors. Many of the answers cite recent related literature, the references for which are located at the back of the manual. These additional citations may also serve as fuel for discussion groups, exam questions, or assignments related to hypothesis testing, experimental design, critical thinking, and so forth.

The second part of each chapter in this manual contains a set of ten multiple-choice questions and five "review and challenge" questions. The multiple-choice questions are derived directly from the chapters of *Principles of Animal Behavior* and thus should be useful for testing students' knowledge of the text. The "review and challenge" questions either ask students to elaborate on the concepts that they learned in each chapter or require students to conduct further research on selected topics in animal behavior. These questions are in essay format, and some might be useful as exam questions, depending on the length of the class period. In addition, the "review and challenge" questions can be used as student-led discussion pieces, individual presentations, or group research projects.

I extend my sincere gratitude to those who awakened my inner-ethologist and to those whose insights were invaluable in the completion of this manual. First and foremost, I thank Lee Alan Dugatkin—a central figure in my development as an experimental biologist, a dear colleague, and an extraordinary mentor—for providing me with the opportunity to collaborate on this textbook-manual fusion. I thank Jack Repcheck, Julia Hines, and Sandy Lifland at W. W. Norton & Company for their patience and significant comments and correspondence regarding this manual. I am also indebted to Larry Wolf (Syracuse University) and Yuying Hsu (National Taiwan Normal University) for encouraging me, as an undergraduate, to pursue a career in animal behavior and for igniting my passion for discovery in the field of ethology. Kristin Bonnie (Emory University and Yerkes Primate Research Center) and Gordon Schuett (Zoo Atlanta, Georgia State University, and Center for Behavioral Neuroscience) offered precious advice on the contents of this manual. And to my beloved family—Richard Earley, Barbara Scavotto-Earley, and Angela Earley—for their perpetual encouragement, support, and understanding. This manual is dedicated to Louis and Carme Scavotto and Roger Kraut—three dear individuals who are simply inspirational!

Ryan L. Earley

| Principles of Animal Behavior

DISCUSSION QUESTIONS

1. Take a few hours one weekend day and focus on writing down all the behavioral observations you've made recently, as well as any, even indirect, behavioral hypotheses you have constructed. Think about your interaction with both people and with nonhumans. How has your very brief introduction into ethology reshaped the way you observe behavior?

As described at the beginning of this chapter, almost everyone has asked questions about animal behavior—sometimes due to interest and other times due to sheer necessity—and this, technically, makes us all ethologists. Nevertheless, understanding the foundations on which **ethology** was built and the ways in which ethological questions are asked makes a world of difference in how inquiries related to animal behavior are posed and interpreted. My first exposure to ethology as an undergraduate student was nothing short of revolutionary. Short flower photography sessions on the banks of a pond turned into extended observation sessions of the animals inhabiting its murky edges. What were once just droves of dragonflies became populations in which there existed individual variation in coloration patterns, choice of locations to deposit eggs, territorial prowess, and so on. An understanding of ethology triggered a greater appreciation for the many facets of individual variation (e.g., behavior, morphology) and also prompted questions about the causes (e.g., development, genetic variation) and the ultimate consequences of variation (e.g., differences in reproductive success or survival). Of course, introductions into ethology may have different impacts on different people in terms of the ways they observe behavior. This first chapter emphasizes natural selection, learning, and cultural transmission as separate, but certainly intertwined, foundations of animal behavior. With an introductory understanding of these three foundations, you are equipped to ask questions about how natural selection could have shaped behavior across generations, how learning can modify behavior within a lifetime, and how cultural transmission can intensify the spread of behavioral traits through a population. In addition, the examples of beak variation in Galápagos finches and xenophobia in common mole rats clearly demonstrate that environmental conditions (e.g., drought vs. rainfall, mesic vs. arid) constitute an important piece of the puzzle in studies of animal behavior. Thus, you should now also be more aware of the environmental theater in which animals behave and how this could affect behavior in the short term or over many generations. Having a basic introduction to ethology and its underlying principles should be like putting on panoramic glasses that expand your appreciation for the complexities of animal behavior and foster the development of rigorous ethological questions and testable hypotheses.

2. Why do we need a science of ethology? What insights does this discipline provide both the scientist and the layperson?

Ethology draws on the principles of a diverse array of fields, from neurobiology to ecology, in order to address questions about how and why animals behave the way they do. Whether questions are tackled observationally or experimentally, the insights gained by studying animal behavior permeate the lives of scientists and nonscientists alike. An exhaustive description of the many reasons why we need a science of ethology would require something akin to a multivolume encyclopedia, but several reasons are highlighted here (Caro, 1998; Dell'omo, 2002; Price, 2003). Veterinary and farming practices are a testament to applied animal behavior in action. The growth and welfare of livestock depend in large part on the implementation of proper housing conditions and feeding regimes, a task that hinges on understanding, for instance, how group size and dominance relationships within the group affect feeding behavior and growth rates. The well-being of your pet depends on your ethological skills (e.g., detecting abnormal behavior) and then on the expert diagnosis of your veterinarian, who must be able to assess and treat behavioral disorders (e.g., stress, excessive aggression). This information is also often disseminated to animal control personnel and may be used in deciding which animal is appropriate for certain tasks—for example, in screening for seeing-eye dogs (see Chapter 17). In addition, trainers draw on the tenets of classical psychology (e.g., positive reinforcement, conditioning) to mold the behavior of household pets. Animal behavior also plays an integral role in field and zoo conservation efforts, recreational fisheries practices, and the development of national and/or state parks. For instance, understanding reproductive and courtship behavior may facilitate captive breeding programs in zoos, while knowledge of feeding behavior and competitive prowess may provide clues as to why non-native species (e.g., zebra mussels in the waterways of the United States) decimate native fauna (e.g., other bivalve mollusks and filter feeders). Changes in the behavior of stream-dwelling animals or the mere presence of some species and absence of others can tell much about water quality, pollutant levels, and ecological disturbances. Familiarity with aggressive behavior and how captive rearing programs and artificial selection influence behavior is essential for the successful integration of fisheries-reared sport fish (e.g., salmonids, centrarchids) with natural populations. Similarly, understanding the home range size, diet, migratory patterns, and social structure of animal species within a community is an important consideration in the design and development of national and/or state parks. Lastly, the interaction of the discipline of animal behavior with neurobiology, endocrinology, and genetics is essential for understanding the molecular underpinnings of certain behavioral disorders (e.g., depression, generalized anxiety disorder, post-traumatic stress disorder) and in developing more effective treatments. All of these examples show that the insights gained by studying ethology are far reaching, impacting progress in scientific fields as different as conservation biology and medicine and influencing the daily lives of nonscientists (e.g., pet owners).

3. *Imagine you are out in a forest, and you observe that squirrels there appear to cache their food only in the vicinity of certain species of plants. Construct a hypothesis of how this behavior may have been the result of (a) natural selection, (b) individual learning, and (c) social learning.*

Caching is a behavior in which animals store provisions for future use. There may be many hypothetical reasons why squirrels cache their food near certain species of plants. Thus, the answers provided here should be considered as only some of the many possibilities. First, let us examine how this type of caching behavior could arise as a result of **natural selection**. Let us assume that at some time in the past substantial variation in caching behavior existed between individuals of this population: some squirrels stored their food in open areas, some cached near grasses, and still others cached near well-foliated plants. You discover that some social animals exhibit cache-raiding behavior—that is, astute observers within the social group will watch where others store their food and subsequently raid the cache for a free meal or for free stores of their own (Bugnyar and Kotrschal, 2002). Suppose that squirrels live in social groups within which individuals have ample opportunity to observe the caching forays of their groupmates. Individuals that cache in open areas or near grasses that provide little cover are easily seen by their cache-raiding conspecifics. Thus, these animals lose much of their food to the thieves and experience low rates of food retrieval. In contrast, squirrels that store provisions near well-foliated plants are able to evade cache-raiders, maintain the secrecy of their cache location, and retrieve a large proportion of the stored food. If squirrels that retrieve a large proportion of their cache survive better over winter, grow faster, and experience competitive or reproductive advantages, then the different caching strategies (e.g., in open areas, among grasses, or near well-foliated plants) have associated fitness consequences. Animals that cache out of view of conspecifics may survive to reproduce multiple times or may be capable of producing many offspring while animals that cache in the open or near grasses either die early or cannot invest as much energy in offspring. Thus, natural selection favors the caching behavior in which food is stored near well-foliated plants (i.e., these animals contribute more offspring to future generations). What you are observing while hiking through the forest is the result of natural selection acting on the different caching strategies; natural selection has shaped behavior such that most animals in the group cache near well-foliated plants. This interpretation assumes that natural selection acted on caching behavior rather than on the ability to learn where to cache food.

If **individual learning** is responsible for the observed caching behavior, then the squirrels' current caching decisions are based on past caching experiences. At a young age, squirrels may store their food in several different locations—in open areas, near grasses, and near well-foliated plants. But, since cache-raiders are present, only the stores located near well-foliated plants will provide a high return. Perhaps the squirrels are able to keep track of how profitable each cache site is in terms of the proportion of provisions retrieved from each location. With experience, squirrels will learn that caching in the open or near grasses is less profitable than caching near well-foliated plants. Thus, the returns of past caching experiences alter future caching decisions. It is important to note that if individual learning mediates caching behavior, all squirrels will not cache near well-foliated plants. Younger or less experienced animals will be more prone to make "mistakes" (e.g., caching in open areas) than older, more experienced squirrels. In this situation, behavioral variation will exist between individuals based on experience and caching behavior will vary within each individual, depending on its age and experience. As stated in the chapter, invoking learning as an explanation does not preclude natural selection; natural selection could favor the ability to learn, while learning itself produces the observed caching behavior.

Lastly, if **social learning** (or cultural transmission) is responsible for caching behavior, then squirrels will observe where conspecifics are storing food and might copy this choice when caching their own food. The propensity to cache food or to learn the location of superior storage sites could have been shaped by natural selection, but rapid transmission throughout the population of information about new caching locations could be achieved through social learning. At one time, the squirrels in this group could have all cached food in open areas, but one squirrel might have deviated from this pattern and stored its food near well-foliated plants. Observer squirrels with no past experience caching near well-foliated plants might copy this behavior and begin to store food in the same manner as the first "demonstrator." In this situation, information is transmitted passively from one individual to the next. It is also possible that the location of caching sites could be transmitted via social learning from parents to offspring in an active fashion analogous to teaching (Chapter 5). Here, one might predict consistent caching behavior within kin groups but not between different kin groups (thus, all individuals in the population would not necessarily cache near well-foliated plants). Crossing kin boundaries, novel food storage behavior could spread through the population quickly. Without emigration from the group, however, this behavior would be unlikely to reach adjacent squirrel populations. Nonetheless, different populations of the same squirrel species living in habitats with similar structures might cache food in similar characteristic locations. With the appropriate empirical tests, one could determine whether population-specific caching behaviors were shaped by cultural transmission or by environmental factors.

4. Why do you suppose that mathematical theories play such a large part in ethology? Couldn't hypotheses be derived in their absence? Why does mathematics force an investigator to be very explicit about his ethological hypotheses?

Theoretical approaches to ethology involve the construction of virtual mathematical worlds in which the investigator examines the influence of a defined set of parameters on, for instance, foraging decisions or dominance hierarchy formation. As described in this chapter, mathematical models often simplify the natural world and its inherent complexities to generate explicit predictions about animal behavior that are applicable across a wide variety of animal systems. Mathematical models sometimes spawn novel predictions that are not entirely intuitive or that call for a restructuring of current hypotheses. Thus, these predictions often serve as the springboard for empirical tests in ethology, as is evident throughout this textbook. The beauty of many mathematical models is their generality and testability. Are the predictions upheld when tested empirically in nature or in the laboratory? If the predictions do not generally apply to the real world, those who are mathematically savvy can revise the assumptions of the model or adjust the parameters used to generate new, testable predictions. Similarly, if a model applies to some animal systems but not to others, new mathematical theories can provide insights into why certain behavioral patterns differ among different species. Thus, although hypotheses can, and often are, developed in the absence of mathematical theory, the predictions of these models can cull the behavioral options or provide novel behavioral alternatives for empiricists to examine.

MULTIPLE-CHOICE QUESTIONS

1. Natural selection is *best* described as a process by which
   a. the frequency of certain traits increases over evolutionary time in a random fashion.
   b. the frequency of traits that confer reproductive and/or survival success increases over evolutionary time.
   c. the frequency of traits that are passed on from one generation to the next increases over evolutionary time.

    d. the frequency of traits that confer reproductive and/or survival success and are passed on from one generation to the next increases over evolutionary time.

    e. the frequency of traits that hinder reproductive and/or survival success and are passed on from one generation to the next increases over evolutionary time.

2. Individual learning and cultural transmission differ in which of the following ways:

    a. Individual learning alters the behavior of an organism within a lifetime, while cultural transmission does not.

    b. Individual learning can lead to the rapid spread of a behavior through a population, while cultural transmission cannot.

    c. Individual learning does not permit the transmission of information across generations, while cultural transmission does.

    d. Individual learning involves copying the behavior of others, while cultural transmission does not.

    e. Individual learning allows behavioral traits to spread quickly through a population both within an organism's lifetime and across generations, while cultural transmission allows behavioral traits to spread through a population only across generations.

3. Xenophobia is defined as the

    a. fear of scarce resources.

    b. fear of arid environments.

    c. fear of disruption of group dynamics.

    d. fear of living underground.

    e. fear of unknown individuals from outside one's group.

4. Which of the following statement(s) are not true:

    a. Learning and natural selection operate independently.

    b. Past experiences can alter behavior within the lifetime of an individual via learning.

    c. The ability to learn can be genetically encoded.

    d. Natural selection can operate on the ability to learn.

    e. Learning can change behavior within a generation, while natural selection can change the frequency of different learning rules across generations.

5. W. D. Hamilton's inclusive fitness hypothesis states that:

    a. Total fitness depends only on the number of viable offspring an individual produces.

    b. Both one's own offspring and the benefits received from helping to raise related offspring contribute to total fitness.

    c. The number of viable offspring sired contributes less to total fitness than the number of related offspring an individual helps to rear.

   d. Total fitness is influenced to a large extent by helping to rear unrelated offspring.
   e. Total fitness is influenced only by the extent to which an individual helps to rear offspring of blood relatives.

6. Conceptual approaches to ethology involve
   a. generating complex mathematical models of the world to establish explicit prediction about animal behavior.
   b. combining ideas from different subdisciplines in a novel way to generate new sets of predictions about animal behavior.
   c. conducting controlled experiments in the field to test hypotheses related to animal behavior.
   d. conducting controlled experimental studies in the laboratory to test hypotheses related to animal behavior.
   e. neglecting past observations and experiments in order to generate novel concepts concerning animal behavior.

7. Which of the following *best* describes the empirical approach to ethology:
   a. Always assume that correlations between two events indicate that one event caused the second event to occur.
   b. Design a series of controlled experiments in the field or laboratory to test an existing theory.
   c. Avoid manipulating ethological or environmental variables in order to conduct a properly controlled study.
   d. Observe animal behavior in a natural setting to uncover interesting trends and use controls or manipulations to determine causality.
   e. Utilize only observational methods to test theories and concepts related to animal behavior.

8. Contemporary ethological experimentation was initiated by which of the following Nobel Prize winners:
   a. R. A. Fisher, John Maynard Smith, and W. D. Hamilton
   b. Niko Tinbergen, R. A. Fisher, and Konrad Lorenz
   c. Karl von Frisch, W. D. Hamilton, and James Watson
   d. W. D. Hamilton, Konrad Lorenz, and R. A. Fisher
   e. Konrad Lorenz, Niko Tinbergen, and Karl von Frisch

9. The three foundations of ethology are
   a. molecular genetics, natural selection, and learning.
   b. neurobiology, anthropology, and psychology.
   c. psychology, learning, and cultural transmission.
   d. cultural transmission, natural selection, and learning.
   e. endocrinology, developmental biology, and natural selection.

10. Peter and Rosemary Grant's work on the Galápagos Islands has shed much light on how natural selection can operate in a natural setting over short periods of time. Which of the following phrases *best* describes the Grants' work on the Galápagos Islands?
    a. There is differential success of species of Darwin's finches with different beak sizes based on the size and abundance of seeds.
    b. Inclement weather patterns directly influence beak size in Galápagos finches.
    c. Finch species with large beaks outcompete species with small beaks when small seeds are abundant.
    d. Finch species with large and small beaks compete only when small seeds are abundant.
    e. Plants with large seeds increase in frequency when large-beaked finches are abundant.

REVIEW AND CHALLENGE QUESTIONS

1. What is the key difference between observational and experimental studies in ethology? What are some possible advantages to each type of study?

2. Can natural selection and learning or natural selection and cultural transmission influence specific behavioral patterns simultaneously? Provide an example demonstrating the possible interactions between natural selection and either learning or cultural transmission.

3. Based on the definitions provided in the text, what are the primary differences between individual learning and social learning?

4. Conceptual advances in ethology often mark the marriage of ideas generated in animal behavior with those of different subdisciplines or even entirely different fields. What do conceptual approaches contribute to ethology? As you become more familiar with the animal behavior literature, can you identify key interactions between different disciplines that have triggered new developments and/or novel ways of thinking about a specific set of behaviors?

5. As a student of animal behavior, you must distinguish between correlation and causation. What types of information can be gleaned from a correlation between two events? How can you establish whether the first event caused the second to occur? As an optional exercise, devise an imaginary correlation between two events relevant to animal behavior. Present this discovery to your classmates and formulate several alternative causal hypotheses (i.e., what else could have caused this event to occur)? Finally, develop an experiment or multiple experiments to test between these alternatives.

ANSWER KEY FOR MULTIPLE-CHOICE QUESTIONS

1.	d	6.	b
2.	c	7.	d
3.	e	8.	e
4.	a	9.	d
5.	b	10.	a

| Natural Selection

DISCUSSION QUESTIONS

1. How was it possible for Darwin to come up with his theory of natural selection in the complete absence of a science of genetics? Many modern studies in ethology rely on genetics, particularly molecular genetics, as a critical tool. How did Darwin manage without this tool?

As an extraordinary naturalist, keen observer, and astute ethologist, Charles Darwin was able to document the astounding **variation** that occurs both within and between species, and the potential **fitness** consequences of this variation. He also recognized that **heritable** traits were essential for natural selection to operate. The following three quotes from *On the Origin of Species* (1859) encompass the prerequisites for natural selection and demonstrate that Darwin stressed the importance of some, yet undiscovered, mode of inheritance:

> Unless favourable variations be inherited by some at least of the offspring, nothing can be effected by natural selection (p. 9)
> The laws governing inheritance are for the most part unknown. No one can say why the same peculiarity in different individuals of the same species, or in different species, is sometimes inherited and sometimes not so. . . . (p. 10)
> . . . we may feel sure that any variation in the least degree injurious would be rigidly destroyed. This preservation of favorable individual differences and variations, and the destruction of those which are injurious, I have called Natural Selection. . . . (p. 63)

By linking variation, competition (e.g., fitness consequences), and some form of inheritance, Darwin came up with his theory of natural selection in the complete absence of a science of genetics. Gregor Mendel's genetic experiments and theories (e.g., principle of segregation) solved the mystery of inheritance and the

Modern Synthesis—a fusion of Darwin's theory of natural selection with genetic modes of inheritance—was born (but not for more than half a century after Mendel's work was published).

2. *Jacques Monod once referred to natural selection as a tinkerer. Why is this a particularly appropriate analogy for how the process of natural selection operates?*

Natural selection is the process by which less fit phenotypes are culled from the population (e.g., by predation events, competition, or failure to reproduce). Thus, only organisms possessing traits that aid in survival and reproductive success are able to contribute to future generations. Natural selection can operate only on existing variability, which may have arisen through any number of mutations, genetic recombination, or migration of new phenotypes (and their underlying genotypes) into the population. Just as a tinkerer is restricted to the parts he has in his workshop, so too is natural selection limited to the variability that exists in nature. Furthermore, just as a tinkerer's creations seem jury-rigged, so too do the products of natural selection. This is because certain pieces that the tinkerer might like to use may only be available to him at certain times, and the same holds true for the process of natural selection. The tinkerer and natural selection alike produce a product that is well designed, but not necessarily aesthetically pleasing.

3. *Read Reeve and Sherman's (1993) paper on "Adaptation and the goals of evolutionary research," in volume 68 (pp. 1–32) of the journal* Quarterly Review of Biology. *After reviewing all the definitions of "adaptation," do you agree with Reeve and Sherman's approach to this subject? If you do not agree, explain why not by listing your reasons.*

Reeve and Sherman's (1993) paper entitled "Adaptation and the goals of evolutionary research" had four main objectives: (a) to critically examine the many definitions proposed for "adaptation," (b) to provide their own conceptual definition of adaptation, one that would incorporate the most powerful aspects of its predecessors, (c) to elucidate the key components of their definition, and (d) to judiciously address the challenges to adaptationism using their proposed definition as a springboard. For purposes of reference, here is an outline of the paper:

a. Past definitions as interpreted by Reeve and Sherman (direct phrases from the paper are in quotations)
   (1) *Historical definition.* An adaptation is defined, generally, based on the original function of a trait rather than the current utility of the trait.
   (2) *Derived-trait definition.* An adaptation is a derived trait—that is, it is a trait that is present in any given species but *not* present in its ancestors.

(3) *Teleonomic definitions.* An adaptation is the product of natural selection and the result of considerable "fine-tuning" over evolutionary time. Teleonomy is defined as "the quality of apparent purposefulness of structure or function in living organisms due to their evolutionary adaptation" (Merriam Webster's Collegiate Dictionary, 11th Edition).

(4) *Sober's definition.* An adaptation is a "trait that must have spread through the action of natural selection."

(5) *Nonhistorical definition.* An adaptation does not rely on an organism's history but rather identifies specific changes to phenotypic characteristics—energy allocation, physiological efficiency, developmental patterns, reproductive rate.

b. Reeve and Sherman's definition of adaptation. An adaptation is a phenotypic variant that results in the highest fitness among a specified set of variants in a given environment.

c. Key features of the Reeve and Sherman definition

(1) *Phenotype-set* is the group of variant phenotypes that can be compared in terms of relative fitness (i.e., their contribution to future generations).

(2) *Fitness measure* is a criterion by which the investigator can estimate the relative fitness of the variant phenotypes (e.g., reproductive success).

(3) *Environmental context* includes all biotic and abiotic factors in the environment that affect the relative fitness of the alternative phenotypes (i.e., those factors that can potentially contribute to variation in fitness among the alternative phenotypes).

d. Challenges to adaptationism

(1) *Phylogenetic inertia* occurs when a trait remains static (i.e., unchanged) over evolutionary time (see Reeve and Sherman for alternative interpretations).

(2) *Genetic correlation* occurs when traits are genetically linked such that positive selection of one of the traits results in the second, linked trait (adaptive or not) appearing in future generations as well.

(3) *Developmental constraints* occur when the kind of alternative phenotypes that can exist within a population are limited by the developmental pathways characteristic of the organism in question.

(4) *Mechanistic explanations* occur when traits arise as a byproduct of some proximate mechanism (see Chapter 3) underlying a different (but possibly related) trait.

The essence of this question is to have you delve into the Reeve and Sherman paper with a critical eye. Investigate past definitions by gathering the relevant literature (see references in Reeve and Sherman's paper) and outline *your* interpretation of each definition; this exercise might best be executed in groups. Discuss previous definitions of "adaptation" with your professor and your classmates and then consider the new definition proposed by Reeve and Sherman to determine whether it provides any advantages over past definitions. Take some time to scrutinize the "challenges to adaptationism," as most provide interesting historical and even current perspectives on the study of adaptation and natural selection. Another helpful exercise might be to peruse recent papers on this topic so as to get a better feeling for where the "adaptation" debate stands (e.g., Allen and Bekoff, 1995; Griffiths, 1996; Crespi, 2000; Debat and David, 2001; Autumn et al., 2002).

4. When considering how much variation in a behavioral trait is genetic and how much is environmental, how does the "uterine environment" complicate matters?

As described in the text, **phenotypic variation** represents the amount of variation in a trait due to genetics *plus* the amount of variation due to the environment. Environmental influences on phenotypic variation can include differences in food availability, temperature, and velocity of water current. Such differences in environmental conditions can yield trait variation. Furthermore, some environmental variance can result from animals of the same species developing in similar environments (as discussed in the "Dissecting Behavioral Variation" section of the text). The uterus constitutes one such shared environment (particularly in eutherian mammals) because many developing embryos are exposed to similar conditions—that is, the internal reproductive environment of the mother. Let's say that during your investigation of how much variation in a behavioral trait is genetic and how much is environmental, you neglect the possibility of "shared uterine environment effects." If the uterine milieu influences variation in any significant way, neglecting this shared environment would necessarily lead to an overestimation of the amount of variation due to genetics. To complicate matters even further, it is possible that the uterine environment does not represent a shared environment at all! Some recent studies suggest that some variation in behavioral and morphological traits (e.g., reproduction, aggression, genitalia) is influenced by whether an individual was positioned near a male or female sibling embryo in utero (see Ryan and Vandenbergh, 2002, for a review; also see Chapter 3 of the text—"Hormones and Proximate Causation").

5. Secure a copy of Gould and Lewontin's (1979) paper, "The spandrels of San Marcos and the Panglossian paradigm: A critique of the adaptationist programme" in volume 205 (pp. 581–598) of the Proceedings of the Royal Society of London, Series B. List both the merits and flaws in Gould and Lewontin's approach to "adaptationist thinking." Overall, do you think their critique is a fair one?

This question has a similar objective as Question 3, namely to familiarize you with some intellectual debates surrounding "adaptation" and the "adaptationist programme" (as Gould and Lewontin have dubbed it). It is essential that you examine this paper with the intent of formulating your *own* ideas about the utility of Gould and Lewontin's critique of adaptationism. To facilitate your plunge into "The spandrels of San Marcos and the Panglossian paradigm: A critique of the adaptationist programme," a brief outline of Gould and Lewontin's major ideas are provided below.

a. How studies on adaptation are conducted

First, Gould and Lewontin argue that organisms should be studied as integrated wholes rather than atomized into discrete traits. Their contention is that an organism is composed of many traits that are inextricably linked to one another. Thus, examining whether each solitary trait is optimally designed by natural selection necessarily undermines the integrated nature of the organism itself. Second, the authors argue that adaptationists are quick to judge nonoptimal traits as resulting from optimal tradeoffs (e.g., traits themselves may be nonoptimal but, tradeoffs between the focal traits and other traits may render the organism, as a whole, best fit) rather than considering options other than that the trait arose through natural selection.

b. How adaptationist arguments are constructed

Here Gould and Lewontin provide several examples of "adaptationist arguments" that they feel fail to consider options other than that the trait arose through natural selection. The lines of argument critiqued by the authors include:
 (1) If one adaptive argument fails, try another.
 (2) If one adaptive argument fails, assume that another must exist.
 (3) In the absence of a good adaptive argument . . . attribute failure to an imperfect understanding of where an organism lives and what it does.
 (4) Emphasize immediate utility and exclude other attributes of form.

c. Alternatives to the adaptationist programme

A significant portion of Gould and Lewontin's paper is dedicated to offering alternatives to "immediate adaptationism for the explanation of form, function, and behavior" (quoted phrase comes directly from the paper; see Reeve and Sherman's 1993 paper for contrasting views). These alternatives include:
 (1) Less fit phenotypes may arise and/or persist due to random processes (e.g., genetic drift).
 (2) The "form" of the trait in question may be a byproduct of selection for another trait; this is similar to the genetic correlation described in the answer to Question 3.
 (3) Situations where the trait itself is modified may not be a consequence of natural selection but rather a response to certain environmental circumstances—phenotypic plasticity.
 (4) Multiple variants may have essentially the same fitness (i.e., multiple adaptive peaks may be achieved).

(5) The current utility of a trait may differ from that for which it arose in the first place and be affected by developmental, architectural, or historical constraints. This represents the crux of Gould and Lewontin's "spandrels" analogy (also see Arthur, 2001, for new perspectives on "constraints").

MULTIPLE-CHOICE QUESTIONS

1. Which of the following factor(s) does *not* generate new variation in a population?
   a. transposition
   b. migration
   c. genetic recombination
   d. heritability
   e. base mutation

2. Quantitative trait loci are *most* useful in the analysis of
   a. traits encoded by the expression of multiple genes.
   b. traits that are heritable.
   c. traits encoded by a recessive allele.
   d. traits encoded by the expression of one gene.
   e. traits encoded by a dominant allele.

3. Which of the following best characterizes eusocial naked mole rats:
   a. many queens and all males are reproductively active; low relatedness
   b. reproductive division of labor without overlapping generations
   c. high relatedness but no communal care of the young
   d. overlapping generations and high relatedness; all colony members reproduce
   e. overlapping generations, high relatedness, and reproductive division of labor

4. Alleles are defined as
   a. genes that require only a single copy to be expressed.
   b. alternative forms or variants of the same gene.
   c. regions of a chromosome containing a set of genes that contributes to the expression of a single trait.
   d. those genes that cannot be subject to natural selection.
   e. genes that require two copies to be expressed.

5. Narrow-sense heritability analysis measures the proportion of variance in a trait attributable to
   a. combined genetic and environmental variance.
   b. environmental variance alone.

    c. that portion of genetic variance accessible to natural selection.

    d. maternal environment effects.

    e. phenotypic variance.

6. Which of the following is *not* required for natural selection to operate:
   a. The resource in question must be limited in some way.
   b. Variation in the trait of interest must exist.
   c. All alleles in the population must be dominant alleles.
   d. Some mode of inheritance must exist.
   e. Traits must influence an individual's relative expected contribution to the next generation.

7. Genetic recombination involves
   a. transposition of a section of DNA from one part of the genome to another.
   b. addition of a single nucleotide to a section of DNA.
   c. replacement of one nucleotide with a different nucleotide.
   d. deletion of a single nucleotide from a section of DNA.
   e. exchange of genetic material between homologous chromosomes during cell division.

8. The phenotype of an organism is defined as
   a. those traits that are coded by recessive alleles.
   b. those traits that are not subject to natural selection.
   c. the genes that an organism possesses.
   d. those traits that are coded by dominant alleles.
   e. the sum of all observable traits including behavior and morphology.

9. Brood parasitism is *best* defined as a situation in which
   a. females transfer their eggs to a nest other than their own, thereby avoiding the costs of parenting.
   b. females transfer parasites to the nests of other females to decrease the viability of competitors' offspring.
   c. parasites are transferred between bird nests that are located in close proximity to one another.
   d. females actively adopt the offspring of related individuals.
   e. females offer their young food items infested with parasites so as to increase offspring immune function.

10. Which of the following represents the result of selection pressures on guppy (*Poecilia reticulata*) populations located in high-predation streams?
    a. fewer and larger offspring per brood
    b. increased growth rates and slower maturation rates
    c. tight schooling behavior and frequent predator inspection
    d. fewer broods of offspring and fast maturation rates
    e. close-range predator inspection and schooling in small groups

REVIEW AND CHALLENGE QUESTIONS

1. Describe at least three prerequisites for natural selection to operate.

2. How would you define "fitness"? Why is it important to examine the fitness of each individual *relative* to others in the population?

3. Describe Gregor Mendel's principle of segregation. Why did Mendel's work in the field of genetics provide a powerful addition to Darwin's theory of natural selection?

4. Describe two methods for measuring narrow-sense heritability. How is narrow-sense heritability fundamentally different from broad-sense heritability?

5. If you were to select an organism in which to study the process of natural selection, what features of the organism's life history and/or environment would factor into your decision?

ANSWER KEY FOR MULTIPLE-CHOICE QUESTIONS

1.	d	6.	c
2.	a	7.	e
3.	e	8.	e
4.	b	9.	a
5.	c	10.	c

| Proximate Factors

DISCUSSION QUESTIONS

1. Make the case that with respect to any particular behavioral trait one can't fully understand ultimate causation without understanding proximate causation and vice versa.

The distinction between proximate and ultimate perspectives in ethology is in the type of questions that a researcher asks. **Proximate** questions attempt to elucidate the mechanisms underlying a particular behavioral trait (e.g., neurobiological, physiological, behavioral). For instance, *how* does an animal escape predation? Or *what* mechanisms trigger predator escape behavior. Answers to these questions could include processing of visual information by the retina, interpretation of the threat by specific regions of the brain, the initiation of a physiological cascade that causes muscle contraction, increased blood glucose, or trial-and-error learning (see Chapter 4). **Ultimate** questions attempt to pinpoint the evolutionary forces responsible for the emergence or maintenance of specific traits. For example, *why* are particular antipredator strategies utilized? If the trait is subject to natural selection, the answer to this question might be that animals using this specific strategy were efficient at deterring (or escaping from) predators and thus survived to reproduce, while animals using different strategies were not as lucky! In other words, animals employing the strategy in question had higher fitness than animals that used other antipredator strategies. Integrating proximate and ultimate questions is essential for gaining a comprehensive understanding of any trait, as was clearly demonstrated by Geoff Hill's research on coloration in the house finch. Without integrating proximate and ultimate perspectives, the factors underlying female choice for brighter males may not have been so cleverly illuminated! Of course, any research endeavor, in any animal system, will benefit from an integrative approach. By doing so, we open each ethological question to a world of possibilities—some of which would not be considered if we approached animal behavior using only one perspective.

2. Find the 1998 special issue of American Zoologist *(vol. 38), which was devoted to proximate and ultimate causation. Choose two different papers in this issue and compare and contrast how they try and integrate proximate and ultimate causation.*

The chief goals of this question are to tantalize your brain with vivid accounts of integrative research in animal behavior and to ignite your critical thinking skills. As you select (and read) two papers from this issue of *American Zoologist*, keep the following questions in mind:

a. Do the authors clearly delineate proximate from ultimate causation when describing the animal system(s) with which they work?

b. What type of proximate explanations do the authors invoke (e.g., behavioral, morphological, physiological, neurobiological)?

c. What types of ultimate questions do the authors pose for the trait(s) in question? For instance, do the authors focus on the relationship between the trait and survivability, lifetime reproductive success, or attractiveness?

d. Have the authors demonstrated convincingly that combining proximate and ultimate approaches to animal behavior can be fruitful?

As a brief introduction to this exercise, consider the papers by Wingfield et al. (1998) and Barlow (1998). Wingfield and colleagues introduce the concept of an "emergency life history stage"—a response to unpredictable environmental events that interrupt an animal's normal activities and cause the animal to shunt its resources (e.g., via changes in behavior or physiology) toward activities essential for survival. They then propose that activation of the hypothalamic-pituitary-adrenal (HPA) axis may initiate the emergency life history stage and provide compelling examples of how glucocorticosteroid hormones, one product of HPA axis activation, are involved in the regulation of behaviors associated with the emergency response (e.g., reproductive suppression, mobilization of energy stores, increased foraging, daytime escape behavior, and recovery). In the concluding remarks, the authors state: "This emergency life history stage may play a major role in maximizing overall lifetime fitness by redirecting individuals away from non-essential activities (such as reproduction) during environmental perturbations." Wingfield and colleagues dedicate the bulk of their paper to proximate causation, that is, to the neuroendocrinological mechanisms underlying an animal's response to unpredictable events. But their concluding paragraph highlights ultimate causation, stating that animals that respond in certain ways to unpredictable events may maximize their fitness in the long term.

Barlow's paper is concerned primarily with the mechanisms associated with mate choice and pair-bond formation in polychromatic Midas cichlids (*Amphilophus citrinellum*). In contrast to the neuroendocrinological approach taken by Wingfield and colleagues, Barlow examined aggressive behavior, body color, and morphological traits as putative proximate cues involved in mate selection and pair-bond establishment and stability. One of the key points in Barlow's paper is that interactions among the many mechanisms underlying mate selection may provide more salient insights than any one mechanism alone. For instance, relative aggression levels, size, and color patterns (gold vs. normal) of *both* the male and the female are all involved in the establishment of successful pair bonds. Throughout the paper, Barlow stresses that investigations of proximate mechanisms often lead to the formulation of more powerful questions regarding ultimate causation. Some of these ultimate questions include: *Why* do females select males with normal, rather than exaggerated, traits? *Why* do these fish pair with mates that have similar coloration patterns? *Why* do males and females select large, aggressive mates?

Wingfield and his colleagues and Barlow tackle proximate causation from different, but equally productive angles (neuroendocrinological versus behavioral/morphological). But their approach to ultimate causation is essentially the same—both papers address the potential fitness consequences of the trait in question (e.g., initiating the emergency life history stage or choosing large, aggressive mates).

3. *The lateral line in fish—a series of sensory hair cells running along the side of the body—appears to be used to detect various forms of motion. How might you experimentally examine whether one proximate explanation for the lateral line is predator detection? Could you then slightly modify your experiment to test the ultimate claim that predator detection via the lateral line has been favored by natural selection?*

The lateral line in fish is made up of a system of receptors, or neuromasts, each of which contains sensory hair cells. These sensory hairs can detect low frequency signals emitted from close range sources—for example, from within one body length of the animal in question (see Popper, 1996, for a review of the lateral line system). One source for these signals may be approaching predators. This brings us to our first proximate question: *How* do fish detect predators? To examine whether the lateral line plays an integral role in predator detection, we could design an experiment where (1) the sensory hair cells are manipulated in ways that would reduce (or abolish) lateral line function, and (2) the predator detection behavior of the manipulated animals is compared to that of nonmanipulated animals. Let us assume that we have access to a certain chemical that temporarily shuts down lateral line function by blocking the ability of the sensory hairs to detect low frequency signals. We then split our lot of experimental fish into two treatment groups: (1) those that are exposed to the sensory blocker, and (2) those that are handled in the same way as the exposed fish *but* are not exposed to the sensory blocker. We then introduce our fish into a seminatural arena where one of its natural predators lurks, and we record several types of behavior associated with predator detection (e.g., time spent orienting toward the predator, latency to escape). If the lateral line is involved in predator detection, we might predict that the animals exposed to the sensory blocker will spend less time orienting toward the predator or exhibit slower escape responses than animals that were not exposed to the sensory blocker. If these predictions were borne out during the experiment, we would have obtained some evidence for the lateral line system as an important proximate mechanism used for detecting predators.

These results leave us with the ultimate question of *why* predator detection via the lateral line has been favored by natural selection. In other words, do individuals with a functional lateral line survive better than individuals that lack this sensory system? To examine this question empirically, the same manipulations as described in the above experiment could be utilized. However, we would now be interested in the survival value of the lateral line. Thus, we could establish groups of fish composed of animals exposed and not exposed to the sensory blocker (all of which have been individually marked for identification purposes). These groups could then be transferred to large, seminatural "pools" with adequate refuge and the natural predator. After a certain period of predator exposure, the groups could be assessed for individual mortality. If the lateral line increases predator detection ability, and thus the probability of survival in habitats where predators are present, then animals that were not exposed to the sensory blocker should have a lower mortality rate than animals whose lateral line was ablated. Of course, this type of experiment would likely only scratch the surface with respect to our understanding the survival value of the lateral line. More rigorous examinations of alternative or complementary hypotheses would also be needed.

4. There has been some discussion, but much less experimental work, on the notion that animals shift the sex ratio of their offspring as a result of the sex ratio of their population. Construct at least three proximate explanations about how such a sex ratio shift might occur.

What mechanisms are involved in sex ratio shifting? *How* do animals shift the sex ratio of their offspring? To answer these questions, let us first refer back to Tim Clutton-Brock's work with red deer (the "Red Deer, Dominance Status, and Sex Ratios" section of the text). Female red deer modify resource allocation (i.e., to female versus male offspring), depending on their social status; low-ranking females invest more in female offspring, while high-ranking females invest more in male offspring. Thus, one proximate explanation for shifts in offspring sex ratio is that females are able to assess their social rank and adjust resource allocation accordingly (note that this explanation does not address *why* females should do this). Now let's consider a situation where the nutritional status of females is compromised due to resource limitation. If female offspring require less investment and, if females can invest only a small amount of their already sparse resource budget in offspring, then we might expect offspring sex ratios to be biased toward females across the board. Here resource limitations imposed by the environment serve as a proximate explanation for modifications in offspring sex ratio. For a different perspective, let us consider a situation in which the physiological milieu of the female allows only certain sperm to penetrate the ovum (this superficially resembles a phenomenon known as "cryptic female choice"; Birkhead and Pizzari, 2002). Imagine that some aspect of the female's reproductive physiology repels sperm with the "Y" chromosome but allows sperm with the "X" chromosome to fertilize the ovum, thus biasing the offspring sex ratio toward females. In this case, the proximate mechanism underlying sex ratio shifts is physiological in nature.

We have identified three potential proximate explanations for sex ratio shifts—behavioral (social status), environmental (resource limitation), and physiological (sperm selection). Although each of these mechanisms *could* explain modification in offspring sex ratio, there are likely to be countless alternative hypotheses. The paucity of empirical data in this field indicates the need for a thorough examination of the many alternatives using experimental and theoretical techniques.

5. Elaborate on how learning itself may be a proximate explanation for certain animal behaviors but how the ability to learn is thought of in ultimate terms.

Individual learning is a process by which past experiences alter current behavior (see Chapter 4). As a budding ethologist studying foraging behavior in birds, you notice that young animals forage in a haphazard way while older animals adopt efficient foraging strategies. You then ask the question: *what* causes the older animals to forage in more efficient ways? After conducting a series of experiments, you determine that an animal's foraging strategy depends in large part on its past foraging experience and, since young animals have less experience, they forage less economically than older animals. What you have done is determine that *learning* is a proximate cause underlying specific foraging patterns in your bird species.

Learning provides a degree of plasticity in any behavioral trait that would not be available if, for instance, the trait was encoded genetically. Imagine that a particular foraging behavior was encoded genetically, such that only slight deviations from a specific foraging pattern occurred (e.g., due to genetic variation within a population). Now, imagine that animals learn to adopt a specific foraging pattern based on past experience in a given set of patches, and that the learning process itself could facilitate changes in the foraging pattern if need be (e.g., if encountering a patch of lower or higher quality than average in unpredictable environments). These two hypothetical situations provide a window for examining ultimate questions about learning. *Why* would the ability to learn be favored?

We might propose that, in dynamic, unpredictable environments, animals that learn about patch quality and adjust their behavior accordingly might fare better than animals that are restricted to a certain set of foraging patterns. Thus, natural selection would favor animals that are capable of learning about their environment. Here, we have provided an *evolutionary* explanation for the ability to learn—that is, we have tackled learning from an ultimate perspective.

MULTIPLE-CHOICE QUESTIONS

1. Which statement best represents a *proximate* explanation for bright plumage (or the choice of bright males)?
   a. Females that mate with brightly colored males produce more viable offspring relative to those that mate with dull males.
   b. Males with bright plumage experience higher reproductive success than males with dull plumage.
   c. Males acquire brightly colored plumage by feeding on carotenoid-based foods.
   d. Males with dull plumage are less conspicuous to predators than bright males.
   e. Females prefer brightly colored males because they receive direct or indirect benefits from doing so.

2. Type C sex determination in reptiles is best characterized as
   a. inheritance of certain sex chromosomes from the mother and father.
   b. high nest temperatures favoring females; low nest temperatures favoring males.
   c. high nest temperatures favoring males; low nest temperatures favoring females.
   d. intermediate nest temperatures favoring males; high and low temperatures favoring females.
   e. females produced at intermediate nest temperatures; high and low temperatures producing males.

3. Which of the following is *not* associated with spatial learning and foraging in honeybees?
   a. Honeybees do not fly directly to the food source when first leaving the hive.
   b. Orientation flights begin when bees are one week old; foraging commences at three weeks of age.
   c. Mushroom bodies of foragers are smaller than mushroom bodies of non-foragers.
   d. Younger bees remain at the nest while older bees conduct foraging flights.
   e. Changes in mushroom body size represent one proximate mechanism for spatial learning in honeybees.

4. Which of the following *best* depicts the initial chain of neuroendocrinological events that occur when an animal is exposed to a stressor?
   a. increased CRH production in adrenal glands → increased glucocorticoid production in the hypothalamus → increased ACTH production in the anterior pituitary gland
   b. increased CRH production in the anterior pituitary gland → decreased ACTH production in the hypothalamus → decreased glucocorticoid production in the adrenal glands
   c. increased CRH production in the hypothalamus → increased ACTH production in the anterior pituitary gland → increased glucocorticoid production in the adrenal glands
   d. increased CRH production in the anterior pituitary gland → increased glucocorticoid production in the adrenal glands → increased ACTH production in the hypothalamus
   e. increased CRH production in the hypothalamus → decreased ACTH production in the anterior pituitary gland → decreased glucocorticoid production in the adrenal glands

5. Neurons possess fibers called dendrites that perform which of the following functions:
   a. They transmit electrochemical information to other cells in the nervous system.
   b. They serve as the "space" between cells into which neurotransmitters are released.
   c. They receive electrochemical information from other cells in the nervous system.
   d. They package neurotransmitters and transport them to the synaptic gap.
   e. They control the number of times a neuron fires depending on stimulus strength.

6. Which of the following statements about Type II males in plainfin midshipman fish (*Porichthys notatus*) is *false*?
   a. Type II males do not build nests.
   b. Type II males are larger than Type I, nesting males.
   c. Type II males are referred to as sneakers because they shed sperm in an attempt to fertilize the eggs of nesting females.
   d. The gonad-to-body ratio of Type II males is nine times greater than that of Type I males.
   e. Type II males do not produce "hums" to court females.

7. All else equal, R. A. Fisher's sex ratio theory predicts that natural selection should favor a sex ratio of
   a. two males: three females.
   b. one male: two females.
   c. three males: two females.

    d. one male: one female.

    e. two males: one female.

8. Which of the following statements about hormones is false?

    a. Hormonal state can affect the strength and form of a behavioral response.

    b. Hormones are secreted by ductless glands, which comprise the endocrine system.

    c. Hyposecretion or hypersecretion of hormones can have dramatic effects on many behaviors.

    d. Hormones can affect the organization of behavior.

    e. Hormones and the endocrine system influence behavior independent of the nervous system.

9. One proximate factor related to ultraviolet vision in zebra finches (*Taeniopygia guttata*) involves

    a. a single amino acid change that alters pigment characteristics.

    b. changes in the curvature of the lens, which helps to filter out certain wavelengths of light.

    c. alterations to retinal structure that inhibit processing of violet pigments.

    d. hormones that trigger the release of ultraviolet pigments from specific brain regions.

    e. a vast number of genetic substitutions, the effects of which have yet to be quantified.

10. Which of the following questions addresses ultimate causation?

    a. How does an animal escape predation?

    b. What neurobiological mechanisms are involved in predator escape behavior?

    c. Why do some animals secrete noxious compounds when threatened by a predator?

    d. What is the anatomical basis for rapid escape behavior?

    e. What types of neuroendocrine changes occur after successfully escaping a predator?

REVIEW AND CHALLENGE QUESTIONS

1. Describe how the "threshold" of a nerve cell relates to its activity and briefly outline how an animal's nervous system responds to stimuli of different strengths.

2. Construct an ultimate explanation for "one-eyed" sleep in mallard ducks based on the description provided in the text.

3. Briefly describe the cascade of neurobiological and physiological events that occur when an animal is exposed to a stressor. How is the stress response a

prime example of the importance of integrating multiple levels of analysis to address a specific set of behaviors?

4. Under what circumstances would you expect ultraviolet vision (or UV reflective patterns) to be favored by natural selection? In designing your answer, think about potential interactions between predator-prey relationships, camouflage, mate choice, and so on.

5. Discuss R. A. Fisher's sex ratio theory and outline some circumstances in which a population may deviate from a 1:1 (male: female) sex ratio.

ANSWER KEY FOR MULTIPLE-CHOICE QUESTIONS

1.	c	6.	b
2.	d	7.	d
3.	c	8.	e
4.	c	9.	a
5.	c	10.	c

CHAPTER 4 | Learning

DISCUSSION QUESTIONS

1. Following up on the "optimal forgetting" study in stomatopods that we discussed in this chapter, can you think of other situations in which it might pay for animals to forget, or at least not act on, information they have obtained? Try and come up with three cases and write a paragraph on each case justifying its selection.

The stomatopod example provided in the text demonstrates how ethologists integrate evolutionary processes and animal learning to ask captivating questions about how memory might be shaped by social and ecological factors. In the case of the mantis shrimp (*Gonodactylus bredini*), forgetting appears to be a function of how long the brood remains within the breeding cavity (e.g., four weeks), and optimal memory span seems to have been shaped by the relative costs and benefits of being aggressive toward a past mate. What other types of situations might be conducive to optimal forgetting? Here, we examine three theoretical possibilities:

a. Fighting experience and molting
You will be introduced to the effects of winning and losing aggressive encounters in Chapter 14. For the time being, let's assume that past winners are more likely to win in the future (*winner effect*) and past losers are more likely to lose in the future (*loser effect*). Let us also assume that the winner and loser effects are mediated by the animals' memory of past encounters (e.g., losers remember how badly they were beaten and opt to withdraw from future contests). Now, let's add a twist to the story. Past experiences should be remembered for only so long as the information remains reliable. If individuals grow over time and if body size correlates well with fighting success, then experience obtained while small may not provide reliable information about the probability of winning contests when large. In animals that molt, body size increases in discrete inter-

vals. If the intervening time period between molts is consistent, then natural selection might favor individuals that devalue past information that was obtained prior to a molt. Animals may use the average inter-molt interval as a conservative estimate of when to refrain from using information obtained in the past. Although this optimal forgetting time might not jive with a simple "forget after each successive molt" algorithm (e.g., individuals who fight late in the molt cycle may experience two molts before forgetting), it is a conservative way to gauge when past experience might become irrelevant as a consequence of post-molt increases in size. This type of optimal forgetting might serve losers better than winners. Thus, we might expect the time course of information devaluation to differ depending on the experiences obtained. Of course, the story would become much more complex if each individual fought more than once or experienced a mixture of wins and losses during the inter-molt interval (see Hsu and Wolf, 1999, for the effects of multiple fighting experiences).

b. Cleaner stations and site fidelity

Coral reefs are a hot spot of fish diversity, and the reef inhabitants exhibit some fascinating interspecific associations. For instance, small cleaner wrasses (*Labroides dimidiatus*) make a living out of removing ectoparasites from other species of fish (clients), some of which could easily indulge in wrasse appetizers! The work of Redouan Bshary has shed some light on why cleaner wrasses would put themselves in so much danger to obtain a meal (Bshary, 2002; Bshary and Grutter, 2002; Bshary and Schaffer, 2002; Tebbich et al., 2002). There are two keys to this story: (1) clients rely on cleaners to remove potentially harmful ectoparasites, and (2) both cleaners and clients keep track of who cheats and who doesn't. For instance, clients that regularly attempt to eat the cleaners are less likely to be cleaned and cleaners that make a habit out of nibbling on clients (instead of the ectoparasites) are visited less often. From the clients' perspective, it pays to remember who the biters are and where they are located. Interestingly, the clients may not need to individually recognize each cleaner but rather could get by with remembering where cooperative cleaners hang out. This is because cleaners tend to remain in certain areas for extended periods of time—that is, cleaners exhibit site fidelity. How does this relate to optimal forgetting? Imagine that, on average, cleaners remain site faithful for one week and then move on to a different area. If a client has a positive experience at one site, then it might pay to remember this site for at most one week. Clients that always visit the same site may be more likely to encounter "newly moved in" cheaters than clients that move between sites on a weekly basis. Thus, natural selection might favor individuals that forget lucrative sites after one week has passed—that way these individuals can move on to different areas and reduce the probability of incurring costs at the hands of cheating cleaners. This system is undoubtedly more complex than has been described here, but it serves as a potential example for selectively advantageous forgetting times.

c. Foraging and prey life span

Imagine a situation where prey items are clumped in space and available for only a limited period of time. For instance, take insects that emerge from their aquatic larval stage in droves but survive for only three days and are patchily distributed (e.g., insects emerge from only certain portions of an aquatic habitat and remain in the riparian areas as adults). Also, let's assume that the insect larvae that inhabit different portions of the aquatic environment emerge at different times, such that the insects are available year round but the locality of dense prey aggregations changes every three days, in accord with the insects' life span. In such a scenario, prey items are always available but are never found in the same locality for an extended period of time. Because each area becomes barren once the insects die off, it may pay predators to remember profitable feeding locations for only a short while—namely, for the average life span of the insects in question (three days). Predators that act on previous foraging information for greater than three days run the risk of encountering barren patches, while those that "forget" previous information and frequently move to fresh patches are more likely to encounter a newly emerged feast. Here, selection for memory lapses related to foraging locality is driven by the average life span of prey items.

2. *Obtain a copy of parts I and II of Tooby and Cosmides's 1989 article "Evolutionary psychology and the generation of culture" in volume 10 (pp. 29–97) of the journal* Ethology and Sociobiology. *After reading this article, explain how "Darwinian algorithms" work and how they relate to our discussion of animal learning.*

In this chapter, the fusion of evolutionary biology and classic psychological paradigms was emphasized as the foundation for our understanding of learning in animal systems. Tooby and Cosmides's (1989) paper complements the chapter in the sense that they accent natural selection as a key evolutionary force in the genesis of psychological phenomena. Although this merger of evolutionary and psychological thought processes had cropped up previously, Tooby and Cosmides's analysis was certainly one of the most comprehensive of its kind. Their main goal was articulated most compellingly on p. 46, where they state:

> The goal of evolutionary theory is to define the adaptive problems that organisms must be able to solve. The goal of psychological theory is to discover the information processing mechanisms that have evolved to solve them. Alone, each is incomplete for the understanding of human nature. Together, they are powerful. . . .

This statement provides the scaffolding for what Tooby and Cosmides refer to as Darwinian algorithms. These algorithms are defined as psychological mechanisms that have evolved via natural selection to solve fitness-related problems that an animal may encounter in its environment. A critical component to the authors' argument, at least in how it applies to humans, is that these mechanisms evolved in the past (e.g., at the dawn of human existence) and that modern behavior can be understood by recognizing how these historical, presumably adaptive, mechanisms interact with contemporary conditions. Darwinian algorithms are shaped via the organisms' interaction with its environment, such that algorithms that increase fitness are selected for and ultimately govern the organisms' behavior. Furthermore, evolutionary dynamics promote adaptive specializations that are tailored toward the organisms' environment or the specific fitness-related problems that must be solved (see the hamadryas vs. savanna baboon example on p. 65 of Tooby and Cosmides's article). More complex problems or those that have more severe fitness consequences should be met with more specialized psychological solutions (or algorithms).

How do Darwinian algorithms relate to learning? In short, algorithms that evolve under certain ecological or social selection pressures may regulate learning capacities or the contextual aspects of learning. In the second part of their paper, Tooby and Cosmides examine one specific behavioral phenomenon—social exchange—from an evolutionary psychological perspective. Here, they define a set of problems associated with social exchange for which natural selection should favor specialized algorithms. For social exchanges to occur, individuals must be able to recognize one another, remember past interactions, and have some way of detecting cheaters, each of which may require specifically tailored algorithms. With respect to the last problem—detecting cheaters—individuals that are capable of identifying, through some psychological mechanism or algorithm, conspecifics that have violated the rules of social exchange (e.g., I scratch your back, but you do not scratch mine in return) may be better off in the long run. After all, associating with cheaters in a cooperative paradigm will never pay off (see Chapter 9)! Recall that learning refers to the process by which enduring changes in behavior occur as a result of past experiences. Darwinian algorithms that facilitate the identification of cheaters through past interactions constitute an important aspect of the social exchange paradigm. In other words, Darwinian algorithms that underlie the ability to learn about the cheating tendencies of others should be selectively advantageous because individuals that possess such psychological detection mechanisms will avoid the costs of associating with noncooperative conspecifics.

In all, the tenets of Tooby and Cosmides's article parallel the emphasis of this chapter on learning. While learning incites changes in behavior within an individual's lifetime, natural selection can act on heritable variation in the *capacity* to learn. According to Tooby and Cosmides, natural selection produces adaptively specialized psychological algorithms that can then guide an animal's learning aptitude.

3. *Read Domjan and Hollis's 1988 chapter "Reproductive behavior: A potential model system for adaptive specializations in learning," which appeared in Bolles and Beecher's book,* Evolution and learning *(pp. 213–237). Then outline how*

classic psychological models of learning can be productively merged with evolutionary approaches to learning.

Domjan and Hollis's (1988) chapter emphasizes that our understanding of learning processes can benefit greatly from (1) examining learning processes in biologically relevant contexts, which may differ across species, with the understanding that natural selection may shape learning trajectories and that ecological and social factors play a key role in determining what to learn and how learning is achieved, and (2) investigating learning from an empirical standpoint, where alternative explanations to learning are given their due course. As a student of animal behavior, you are encouraged to read Domjan and Hollis's (1988) chapter with a keen eye so as to determine what you think are the authors' key points. We will touch on a couple of points that emphasize how classic psychological models of learning can be merged with evolutionary approaches. First, Domjan and Hollis propose that animal systems should adhere to two criteria if they are to be amenable to evolutionary analyses of learning: (1) ". . .the response system [the behavior in question] should be one that is either shaped directly by natural selection or is closely related to a directly shaped selection system. If a response system is shaped directly by natural selection, learning mechanisms involved in that response system may also be subject to natural selection," and (2) ". . . the response system should have . . . species specificity and diversity." These two criteria highlight the point that natural selection can act on the capacity to learn and that different selection pressures inherent across ecological conditions may favor different types of adaptive learning specializations. This sets the stage for integrating classic psychology with evolutionary approaches.

One of the major take-home messages from this chapter is that, when applying classical psychological paradigms (e.g., operant or classical conditioning) to study learning, one must do so in a biologically relevant fashion. For instance, if you are examining whether an animal learns to exhibit behavior X when it is followed by a positive stimulus Y, then behavior X and positive stimulus Y should be linked in some biologically relevant way. Take the stickleback example provided in the chapter. Sticklebacks that bit the end of a rod were rewarded by the presentation of a sexually receptive female. If the sticklebacks learn to couple these two stimuli (rod and female), then we might expect the sticklebacks to increase biting behavior over time so as to gain access to reproductive opportunity. However, the sticklebacks did not increase biting behavior. Can we then conclude that sticklebacks are incapable of learning? Or should we conclude that biting is somehow discordant with courtship (e.g., biting may deter females) and that our learning paradigm does not provide a stimulus pair that facilitates learning? Based on the fact that sticklebacks learned to bite the rod more fervently when the stimulus was a male conspecific (which usually elicited aggression), the second option seems more applicable. The second take-home message from this chapter is that learning studies should be subject to the same alternative hypothesis testing rigors as ethological work in other areas. For instance, one must consider several possible unconditioned responses to a conditioned stimulus before assigning learning as the proximate mechanism involved in behavioral changes. Lasting changes in neuroendocrine systems (e.g., changes in hormone titers, receptor densities), which may influence subsequent behavior, may give the false impression that learning has occurred (also note that learning likely has a neuroendocrine component). Domjan and Hollis (1988) provide an intriguing account of how classic psychological paradigms can be merged with evolutionary interpretations of animal behavior. They consider the primacy of evolutionary forces in giving rise to adaptive learning specializations and caution against considering learning as a "black box" that is not influenced by an animal's environmental milieu and ultimately by natural selection.

4. Design an experiment that can distinguish between the two alternative explanations for interpopulational differences in dove foraging, as described in Carlier and Lefebvre's 1996 "Differences in individual learning between group-foraging and territorial Zenaida doves," which appeared in volume 133 (pp. 1197–1207) of the journal Behaviour.

In the "Learning, Foraging, and Group Living in Doves" section of this chapter, you were introduced to an experiment conducted by Carlier and Lefebvre (1996) on differences in learning in group-foraging populations as opposed to territorial populations of Zenaida doves. The authors demonstrated that doves from the group-foraging populations learned faster and were able to learn more complex tasks than doves from the territorial populations. Carlier and Lefebvre conclude that population differences in learning could be accounted for by differences in resource distribution at the two sites. When food resources are abundant but unpredictable, group foraging might be the best option; successful group foragers might rely on rapid information acquisition about patch quality, which could facilitate enhanced learning skills. When resources are limited but predictable (spatially and temporally), territoriality might be the best option; successful territory holders might rely more on adopting efficient defense tactics than on fine-tuning their learning skills. The authors also argue that the learning differences they uncovered were likely not due to natural selection acting on each population to produce adaptive learning specializations, particularly given that there was sufficient genetic "mixing" between the two Zenaida dove populations.

Based on the authors' arguments, two intriguing hypotheses for between-population learning differences remain: (1) individual doves in different environments adjust their behavior to accommodate prevailing local-ecological circumstances (e.g., resource distribution and ensuing social organization), and (2) natural selection has favored adaptive specializations in the two populations, yielding divergent learning curves. How can we discriminate between the "learning during a lifetime" hypothesis (1) and the "adaptive specialization" hypothesis

(2)? One of many potential experiments could involve cross-fostering, a technique commonly used for examining the effects of an animal's environment on the expression of behavior (see "Song Learning and Mate Choice in Cowbirds" in Chapter 6 of the text). Our cross-fostering experiment would entail switching the eggs of doves from the group-foraging population with the eggs of doves from the territorial population. By doing so, we can be relatively confident that the young doves have not yet had the opportunity to learn about their environment. If "learning during a lifetime" shapes the doves' ability to conduct complex learning tasks, we might predict that the cross-fostered young from the group-foraging population would exhibit similar learning curves to those of the individuals from the territorial population (in which they now reside), and vice versa. If natural selection produced adaptive specializations in each dove population, we might not expect the cross-fostering experiment to have much of an impact on the learning curves of the individuals that were switched between populations. Carlier and Lefebvre's fascinating paper and our follow-up experiment touch on the crux of this chapter on learning—that is, how drawing on past experience can adjust individual behavior during a lifetime and how natural selection can shape the propensity to learn.

MULTIPLE-CHOICE QUESTIONS

1. Sensitization is the process by which
   a. animals become less likely to exhibit a response to a stimulus over time.
   b. learning to associate one CS with a US blocks the ability to associate another CS with the same US.
   c. one event predicts the occurrence of a second event.
   d. animals become more likely to exhibit a response to a stimulus over time.
   e. one event predicts that a second event will not occur.

2. Appetitive stimulus is to excitatory conditioning as _____ is to _____.
   a. sensitized stimulus; habituation.
   b. classical conditioning; instrumental conditioning.
   c. blocking; positive reinforcement.
   d. negative stimulus; operant conditioning.
   e. aversive stimulus; inhibitory conditioning.

3. Which of the following statements or phrases is *not* associated with the law of effect?
   a. instrumental conditioning and operant responses
   b. second-order classical conditioning
   c. Associations between stimulus and response are strengthened if the response to a stimulus is followed by a positive reinforcer.

   d. Thorndike's early work on instrumental learning in cats using puzzle boxes.
   e. Associations between stimulus and response are weakened if the response to a stimulus is followed by a negative reinforcer.

4. Learning is *best* defined as
   a. a process by which only aversive stimuli elicit changes in behavior.
   b. changes in behavior that result from past experience.
   c. a permanent change in behavior resulting from hormonal but not neurobiological changes.
   d. a relatively permanent change in behavior as a result of experience.
   e. a process by which only positive stimuli elicit changes in behavior.

5. An unconditioned stimulus is a stimulus that
   a. an animal habituates to immediately.
   b. fails to elicit a response unless associated with a second stimulus.
   c. reinforces certain behavioral responses.
   d. inhibits an animal from performing certain behavioral responses.
   e. elicits a response in the absence of training.

6. When psychologists construct extinction curves, they are examining
   a. the life span of the organism in question.
   b. how long an animal recalls associated events when continuously exposed to paired stimuli.
   c. the strength of an animal's behavioral response to instrumental conditioning.
   d. how long an animal remembers a paired association once the pairing has stopped.
   e. how long it takes for sensitization to occur.

7. Phenotypic plasticity refers to the ability of an organism to adopt
   a. alternative phenotypes depending on environmental and/or social conditions.
   b. many different phenotypes simultaneously.
   c. different morphological phenotypes with no change in behavioral phenotype.
   d. different behavioral phenotypes with no change in morphological phenotype.
   e. one specific phenotype that is fixed throughout the organism's lifetime.

8. David Stephens's model of learning and environmental stability predicts that learning will be favored when environmental predictability is
   a. low within an individual's lifetime but high between generations.
   b. high within an individual's lifetime and between generations.
   c. high within an individual's lifetime but low between generations.

    d. low within an individual's lifetime and between generations.

    e. intermediate within an individual's lifetime and high between generations.

9. Instrumental conditioning involves
    a. providing positive reinforcement only during conditioning.
    b. pairing of an unconditioned and conditioned stimulus.
    c. habituating the subjects to certain stimuli.
    d. preventing the animal from performing specific behaviors during the conditioning process.
    e. positive and/or negative reinforcement of a behavioral response.

10. Which of the following scientists revolutionized the field of instrumental learning by developing the free-operant procedure?
    a. B. F. Skinner
    b. Ivan Pavlov
    c. Edward Thorndike
    d. John Garcia
    e. Harry Harlow

REVIEW AND CHALLENGE QUESTIONS

1. Discuss the general differences between Pavlovian (classical) conditioning and operant conditioning. In terms of what we can glean about animal learning, what are some similarities and differences between these two conditioning paradigms?

2. Why were Garcia's studies on rats in the mid-1960s important for initiating the study of learning from an evolutionary perspective?

3. What types of environs would be conducive to natural selection favoring the ability to learn? Discuss your answer in terms of David Stephens's dichotomy between within- and between-lifetime environmental stability.

4. In this chapter, you were introduced to the relationship between parental investment and between-sex differences in learning. Under what parental investment conditions should females and males have equal ability to learn? When should females exhibit greater learning abilities than males? When should males exhibit greater learning abilities than females?

5. When conducting laboratory studies on animal learning, what sorts of precautions should you take to ensure that your interpretations of the role of learning in your animal system are accurate? If you were not studying learning, why should you remain cognizant of the learning abilities of your study organism?

ANSWER KEY FOR MULTIPLE-CHOICE QUESTIONS

1.	d	6.	d
2.	e	7.	a
3.	b	8.	c
4.	d	9.	e
5.	e	10.	a

| Social Learning and Cultural
Transmission

DISCUSSION QUESTIONS

1. Why do you suppose it took so long for ethologists to focus on the possibility that cultural transmission was an important force in animals? Can you imagine any biases—scientific, ideological, etc.—that could be responsible for this?

Although there are likely to be a variety of reasons why it took so long for **cultural transmission** to be recognized as an important force in nonhuman animals, we will focus on one important factor. Historically speaking, humans (scientists included) have searched far and wide for features that distinguish our species from the other species inhabiting this planet. Not too long ago, tool use was thought to be a defining characteristic of human societies, but we now understand that both avian species and nonhuman primates are capable of tool use (Weir et al., 2002). The existence of culture had, until recently, been defined as a uniquely human characteristic. Presumably, with the belief that humans *must* be different from other animals came some trepidation about assigning culture to nonhuman species. As described in this chapter, however, this chasm has been bridged, and we now have powerful evidence that culture may infuse the societies of animals as diverse as fish and primates! This is not to say that all animals have the same capacity for culture. Indeed, a recent paper by Van Schaik et al. (2003) describes several elements of culture (e.g., innovative displays, the use of symbolic elements). The presence or absence of these elements may be used to define the level of culture achieved in a given animal system. Furthermore, empirical research can test for different cultural elements and thus can provide a rigorous scientific basis for supporting the existence, not of culture itself, but of different aspects of culture in different animal species.

2. Suppose I run an experiment in which I take a bird (the observer) and let him view another bird (the demonstrator) opening a sealed cup by pecking at the circle on the cover of the cup. I then test the observer and see that he now opens the cup by pecking at the circle. What can I infer about social learning here? What other critical treatment is missing from this experiment?

The way to think critically about this question is to ask yourself: If I read a paper where only this one experiment was conducted *and* the authors claimed to have demonstrated social learning, would I be convinced? The answer to this question should be a resounding *no!* Although the experiment described above would certainly be a stepping stone for gauging the potential for social learning in these birds, it by no means rules out alternative hypotheses. It is possible, for instance, that each bird (first, the demonstrator, and next, the observer) figured out how to open the sealed cup independent of any information gained by watching conspecifics—that is, each bird may have come up with the same solution via individual learning. Thus, we need to design an additional experimental treatment that will allow us to rule out this alternative hypothesis.

To start with, determine the variables associated with the treatment described above—the presence of a conspecific, the presence of a sealed cup with a circle on the cover, and the potential for the demonstrator to peck at the cup. Which of these variables should we manipulate in our new treatment? Given that we are interested in testing whether observing the demonstrator peck at the cup influences the bystander's subsequent behavior, we might want to manipulate the ability of the demonstrator to peck at the cup. In our new treatment, the observer would be exposed to a demonstrator and to a cup in the demonstrator's arena. But in this new treatment, the cup will be placed behind a clear glass partition such that the demonstrator cannot exhibit pecking behavior. We can now subject our observer birds to one of two treatments: (1) watch demonstrators successfully open the cup by pecking at the circle, or (2) watch a demonstrator who does not exhibit such behavior. Following these observation sessions, we can place the same type of cup in the observer's arena. If the observer successfully opens the cup in treatment 1 but fails to open the cup in treatment 2, then we might conclude that watching conspecifics (and thus, social learning) is important for cup-opening behavior in these birds. But if the observer successfully opens the cup in both treatments, we might reject social learning as an important mediator of cup-opening behavior. If the observers are able to figure out how to open the cup in both treatments, however, it is possible that prior observation could have increased the speed at which success is achieved. If this turns out to be the case, then we might conclude that social learning and individual learning interact to increase the efficiency of problem solving in our birds. Can you think of any additional treatments that might shed light on the ability of our birds to learn socially (see the "Social Learning and Foraging" section of Chapter 10)?

3. Imagine that adults in some population of monkeys appeared to pick up new innovations (for example, potato washing, stone play) from observing others. How might you disentangle vertical, horizontal, and oblique cultural transmission as possible explanatory forces?

The essential difference between **vertical**, **horizontal**, and **oblique** cultural transmission lies in who transmits information to whom. Recall that vertical cultural transmission entails parents passing information on to offspring, horizontal transmission involves the exchange of information among individuals in the same age class (or cohort), and oblique transmission entails adults passing information along to younger individuals that are not their offspring. Kawamura (1959) observed Imo's sweet-potato-washing innovation and subsequently observed the spread of this behavioral trait throughout the troop of macaques. Despite documenting Imo's innovation and the relatively rapid pace at which other troop members adopted potato-washing behavior, the question of which mechanism(s) drove cultural transmission (e.g., vertical, horizontal, or oblique) still remained. The best way to disentangle these mechanisms in monkey troops, without disturbing natural habits, would be to conduct long-term observational studies in the field, which of course would require a hefty workload, many reliable assistants, and lots of patience! Let's say that you are up for this challenge, and that your monkey troop is particularly innovative (i.e., you'll have ample opportunity to figure out which mechanisms are at work). To begin, you will need to gather information about the demographics (e.g., age classes) of your monkey troop and determine familial relationships. This will allow you to assess the extent to which offspring observe parents, young monkeys observe nonparental adult monkeys, or peers observe peers. Furthermore, you will need to record specific instances of observation, the behavior of the demonstrator, and any novel behavioral changes that occur as a result of observation (e.g., behaving in ways that mimic the behavior of the demonstrator). Over time, you will likely collect enough observational data to bog down even the most "user-friendly" spreadsheet! Nevertheless, these data may provide powerful clues to the mechanisms of cultural transmission. You can reveal these trends by examining associations between the identity of the observer and the demonstrator, the type of innovation being observed, and any changes in behavior that the observation may elicit. You may find that innovative behaviors are transmitted via only a single route (e.g., from parent to offspring), suggesting a critical role for one cultural transmission mechanism (e.g., vertical) in the spread of novel behavioral traits. Or you may find that different types of behavioral innovations are transmitted via different routes (e.g., some from peer to peer and others from old to young), indicating the possibility of context-dependent cultural transmission mechanisms.

4. List the pros and cons of Caro and Hauser's definition of teaching. How might you modify this definition to address what you listed on the "con" side of your ledger?

Caro and Hauser's comprehensive review on **teaching** in nonhuman animals provides a number of captivating examples of how information is transferred from experienced individuals to naive conspecifics (often offspring). Much of their discourse reviews anecdotal and quantitative evidence for teaching in animals, and many of these examples demonstrate that the instructor doesn't simply provide the answer to its pupils but rather coaxes or coaches the recipient to behave in the appropriate ways. In like fashion, rather than providing a definitive "answer" as to whether teaching takes place in the many animal systems described by Caro and Hauser, we encourage you to use critical thinking skills to outline and critique Caro and Hauser's review. You may also search for some recent literature on this topic so as to examine how research on teaching in nonhuman animals has progressed over the past ten years or so. An interesting starting point might be to look at a recent issue of *Brain and Behavioral Sciences* (vol. 24, issue 2, pp. 309–360), which includes a review article on cetacean culture by Rendell and Whitehead (2001) and many commentaries on this article.

Caro and Hauser's definition of teaching is provided on pp. 158–159 of the text and will not be restated here. One of the key positive aspects of the authors' definition is that it allows behavioral ecologists to distinguish teaching from an array of other social learning mechanisms that might, at first glance, be confused with teaching. For instance, they stipulate that teaching requires that individuals modify their behavior in the presence of naive *but not* experienced conspecifics, and this helps to differentiate between social learning and teaching. Furthermore, by proposing that instructors receive no immediate benefit from transmitting information to naive conspecifics, we are able to discriminate between teaching and other types of behavior where information is passed from one individual to another (e.g., aggressive interactions wherein the winner benefits immediately from chasing a conspecific away from a resource). A second interesting positive aspect of Caro and Hauser's definition is that it does not require teaching to involve complex cognitive abilities (e.g., intentionality). Although the authors acknowledge that complex cognitive processes would certainly increase the efficacy of teaching, such processes are not a prerequisite for teaching to occur. Rather, Caro and Hauser astutely recognize that natural selection should favor teaching if teaching provides some delayed benefit to the instructor that in the long run exceeds the sometimes substantial associated costs (e.g., enhancing the skills of kin may increase the teacher's inclusive fitness and may outweigh energetic costs; see Chapter 8). Aside from the two components discussed above, Caro and Hauser's definition includes the following key elements:

a. Instructors should modify their behavior for the benefit of the student.

b. The student should have no experience with the skill or information being transmitted by the teacher.

c. The students should experience some benefit from being taught (e.g., skills that they did not have before or that they would have acquired much later had it not been for the instructor); quantifying these benefits is critical for understanding the selection pressures underlying teaching behavior.

d. The teacher should accrue an immediate cost (but not an immediate benefit) by instructing.

After clarifying many of the terms put forth in their definition, Caro and Hauser proceed to cite compelling examples of putative teaching in nonhuman animals. These examples touch on many of the behaviors that you will learn about as you read this book, including foraging in juncos; hunting in killer whales, cheetahs, and osprey; antipredator behavior in vervet monkeys; tool use in chimpanzees; and singing in cowbirds. One potential downside to Caro and Hauser's definition is that most existing examples of teaching do not entirely fulfill the authors' definition, which brings up some important questions for you to consider. Why do these examples fail to support Caro and Hauser's definition of teaching? Could it be that the authors' definition is too exclusive? Or could it be that no formal definitions of teaching existed in the behavioral ecological literature when these studies were conducted, which limited the empirical rigor with which teaching could be addressed? What elements might be lacking from these examples?

Finally, Caro and Hauser elucidate some central issues in the study of teaching that should be incorporated into future research programs. First, the authors distinguish between opportunity teaching (e.g., placing the naive individual in a situation conducive to learning new skills) and coaching (e.g., using encouragement and punishment to reinforce the use of appropriate behaviors). Second, they distinguish between situations where a teacher changes its behavior in accordance with the pupil's skill level (flexible teaching) and situations where a teacher behaves in similar ways irrespective of the pupil's skill level (fixed teaching). The authors discuss the benefits and costs of flexible versus fixed teaching strategies, and they recognize the important role of an animal's environment (social or physical) in mediating the emergence of such strategies. Third, the authors provide an in-depth treatment of why complex cognitive mechanisms are conducive to but not necessarily paramount to the teaching process. All in all, Caro and Hauser's review should prove to be a stimulating read and will certainly provide enough ammunition for productive discussions regarding the pros and cons of their proposed definition.

5. Suppose that after extensive observations, you determine that certain animals in a population appear to use social learning skills much more often than other individuals and that such differences are due to genetic differences. How might you use the truncation selection technique described in Chapter 2 to examine the narrow-sense heritability of the tendency to employ social learning?

Imagine that we are working with a large population of animals in which social learning skills are easily quantified using some sort of scoring system. For instance, individuals who use their social learning skills most frequently obtain a score of 100, while individuals who lack social learning skills are assigned a score of 0. For the sake of simplicity, let's assume that: (1) we have scored all individuals in the population, (2) score variability in males is similar to that of females—that is, there are no sex-based differences in social learning, and (3) the distribution of scores is bell-shaped with a mean of 50. Our mean score value is labeled x_0. Next, we *truncate* the population by separating males and females that score above 70—these are skillful social learners—from the remainder of the population. Let's say that the average social learning score of these skilled individuals (x_1) is 90. Based on the mean scores of our initial population and the truncated population, we can calculate the **selection differential (S)**, which is simply the difference between x_1 and x_0 (in this case, 40). We then allow the males and females of our truncated population to mate amongst themselves, producing second-generation offspring. After countless hours of experimental testing, we determine the average social learning scores for the individuals in generation 2 (x_2) to be 73. To determine the **response to selection (R)**, we subtract the mean of our initial population from the mean of our population in generation 2 $(x_2 - x_0 = 73 - 50 = 23)$. Narrow-sense heritability for social learning skills in our hypothetical population is then calculated as the response to selection (R = 23) divided by the selection differential (S = 40). Thus, narrow-sense heritability turns out to be 0.58. Compared to most studies on heritability, our narrow-sense heritability coefficient is extraordinarily high, suggesting that the *ability* to learn socially has a significant heritable genetic component. To stimulate some further brain activity, consider the following:

a. Instead of dealing with the lump sum of all social learning activities, you partition social learning skills into specific behavioral subcategories such as "copying the mate choice of others," "imitating vocalizations of nearby conspecifics," "foraging in areas where other foragers are already present," and so on. After conducting rigorous truncation selection experiments, you find that, when taken alone, none of these traits has a significant heritable component. In light of what you found in your original experiment, how would you interpret these results?

b. What might you expect, in terms of your heritability coefficient (R/S), if you truncated only one sex from your original population (e.g., allowing skillful males to mate with females that vary in their social learning skills, or vice versa)?

MULTIPLE-CHOICE QUESTIONS

1. Horizontal cultural transmission refers to a situation in which information is passed
   a. specifically from mother to daughter.
   b. directly from parent to offspring.
   c. between individuals of the same age class.
   d. from adults to unrelated offspring.
   e. between individuals of different species.

2. Which of the following statements *best* describes the relationship between genetic evolution and cultural evolution?
   a. Neither genetic evolution nor cultural evolution can have a dramatic influence on the phenotype of an organism within a lifetime.
   b. Phenotypic effects of cultural evolution can be witnessed within a lifetime or within a few generations while the phenotypic effects of genetic evolution occur less rapidly.
   c. Both processes must operate for tens of thousands of generations for observable phenotypic effects to arise.
   d. Cultural evolution occurs far less quickly than genetic evolution.
   e. Phenotypic effects of both cultural evolution and genetic evolution are almost always evident within the lifetime of an organism.

3. Copying refers to a form of social learning in which
   a. an observer repeats the behavior exhibited by a model individual.
   b. an observer acquires a novel response by witnessing a demonstrator exhibit that response.
   c. the mere presence of a model individual facilitates learning in other individuals.
   d. the performance of an instinctive pattern of behavior in one individual acts as a releaser for the same behavior in other individuals.
   e. observers are drawn to an area containing other individuals and subsequently learn on their own.

4. Which of the following statements does *not* apply to Caro and Hauser's definition of teaching?
   a. The observer must be naive.
   b. Teaching provides immediate benefits for the teacher.
   c. The observer may acquire knowledge earlier in life when taught.
   d. The teacher accrues some costs by modifying its behavior.
   e. The observer may learn skills that would never have been acquired in the absence of teaching.

5. Cultural transmission can be partitioned into which of the following two major subcategories?
   a. contagion and local enhancement
   b. copying and social learning
   c. social learning and teaching
   d. teaching and imitation
   e. teaching and social facilitation

6. Social learning, tool use, and innovation in primates are
   a. negatively correlated with executive brain volume corrected for body size.
   b. positively correlated with absolute executive brain volume.
   c. negatively correlated with body size.
   d. positively correlated with executive brain volume corrected for body size.
   e. positively correlated with body size corrected for executive brain volume.

7. Which of the following individuals is credited as being one of the first to consider that cultural transmission plays an important role in animal life?
   a. W. D. Hamilton
   b. Charles Darwin
   c. R. A. Fisher
   d. George Romanes
   e. Gregor Mendel

8. Culture is *best* defined as
   a. a process by which past experience modifies current behavior.
   b. a means by which information is transmitted between individuals in primate groups.
   c. the transfer of information from experienced individuals to naive individuals.
   d. the genetic transmission of traits across generations.
   e. a system of information transfer that influences an individual's phenotype.

9. Whitehead's research on matrilineal species of whales led to which of the following postulations?
   a. Genetic and cultural transmission cannot interact in shaping animal behavior.
   b. Mitochondrial DNA variation is somehow linked to cultural variation in a manner akin to linkage disequilibrium.
   c. Dialects used in whale vocal communication are under strict genetic control.
   d. All cultural variants and mitochondrial DNA varieties have the same effect on whale fitness.
   e. Culture plays a minor role in the transmission of song dialects relative to genes.

10. Which form of cultural transmission is operating when information is transferred across generations, but not via parent-offspring interactions?
    a. oblique cultural transmission
    b. vertical cultural transmission
    c. altruistic cultural transmission
    d. horizontal cultural transmission
    e. nepotistic cultural transmission

REVIEW AND CHALLENGE QUESTIONS

1. Describe at least two important differences between individual learning and social learning (or cultural transmission). Based on these differences, do you think social learning is unique unto itself or just a special case of individual learning? How would you support your stance on this issue?

2. What features distinguish teaching from social learning? As described in the text, teachers may incur some cost while transmitting information to their off-spring. Can you think of any costs that demonstrators may incur as a result of social learning?

3. As a key part of your development as an ethologist (or behavioral ecologist), you should fine-tune your critical thinking skills such that you are able to identify the assumptions underlying the studies that you read about. Throughout the course of this book, you should have the opportunity to read papers that cover a diverse array of topics, including foraging, kinship, cooperation, and aggression. In doing so, ask yourself the following questions: Have the assumptions underlying some of the key concepts in behavioral ecology gone untested? Are some of these assumptions so seemingly obvious that rigorous empirical tests of these assumptions have been neglected? In cases where ostensibly obvious assumptions have been tested, are they supported? Describe at least one instance where an author has challenged untested assumptions and found that they might not be as obvious as one would be led to believe.

4. Compare and contrast the five different forms of social learning described in this chapter—local enhancement, social facilitation, contagion, imitation, and copying.

5. In the "Modes of Cultural Transmission" section of this chapter, you were introduced to an experiment conducted by Laland and Williams (1998) that suggested that even maladaptive information could be transmitted culturally. Outside of a laboratory setting, do you think maladaptive information could be perpetuated through mechanisms of cultural transmission? In addition, devise a scenario that describes how the transfer of inaccurate or dangerous information might be avoided based on the social learning strategies adopted by a given set of animals.

ANSWER KEY FOR MULTIPLE-CHOICE QUESTIONS

1.	c	6.	b
2.	b	7.	d
3.	a	8.	e
4.	b	9.	b
5.	c	10.	a

| Sexual Selection

DISCUSSION QUESTIONS

1. Suppose that a group of males engaged in a series of fights and that male A emerged as the dominant individual. Now suppose that a female assessed all the males involved in fights and chose male A. Why might this example blur the distinction between intrasexual selection and intersexual selection?

Recall that **intrasexual selection** involves competition among individuals of one sex for access to mates. Conversely, **intersexual selection** entails one sex choosing mates of the other sex based on some criteria reflective of mate quality (e.g., the mates' ability to provide either direct or indirect benefits). In the example provided above, males engage in fights presumably over access to receptive females. Taken alone, this sort of competition qualifies as intrasexual selection. To complicate matters, the focal female chooses the dominant male, possibly because achieving dominance status reveals something about the quality of male A (e.g., physical prowess, ability to defend the young). In this sort of system, where females prefer males that are the best competitors, it is difficult to disentangle whether male-male competition or female mate choice drives sexual selection, particularly if traits that enhance contest success also attract females.

This question should not be misconstrued as meaning that male-male competition and female mate choice *must* be mutually exclusive; it does *not* mean that only one of the two options can mediate sexual selection. Several experimental studies have aimed at testing the relative importance of intrasexual and intersexual selection, thereby recognizing that each can play an integral role in the process of sexual selection (Berglund and Rosenqvist, 2001; Sih et al., 2002). Furthermore, interactions between male-male competition and female mate choice (e.g., when dominant males "override" female mate choice by excluding subordinates from mating opportunities) and the possibility that intersexual and intrasexual selection can act in opposing directions (e.g., when traits that enhance contest success do not indicate male quality) have been examined experimentally (Qvarnstrom and Forsgren, 1998; Nilsson and Nilsson, 2000). Some studies have also demonstrated that intervening factors such as resource abundance can mediate the relative importance of male-male competition and female mate choice in sexual selection (Forsgren et al., 1996). Lastly, it is important to note that females may incite competition among males as a means by which to determine male quality, as was discussed in the "Male-Male Competition by Interference" section of the chapter. Each of these examples demonstrates that (1) it is often difficult to tease apart intrasexual selection from intersexual selection, and (2) in many cases, both male-male competition and female mate choice shape the process of sexual selection.

2. Secure a copy of Kirkpatrick and Ryan's 1991 paper "The evolution of mating preferences and the paradox of the lek" in Nature *(vol. 350, pp. 33–38). Drawing from this paper, list the similarities and differences between sexual selection models in terms of both assumptions and predictions.*

Kirkpatrick and Ryan's seminal paper on sexual selection focuses on the avenues through which female mate preferences evolve. They begin their paper by establishing a null model in which some sort of equilibrium is obtained. Equilibrium refers to a situation in which the establishment of a specific female preference precludes alternative preferences from evolving. In other words, all females in the population do best by preferring certain traits, and this preference remains stable over time. Kirkpatrick and Ryan then introduce familiar models of sexual selection and focus primarily on the differences between models that invoke direct selection versus indirect selection. To compare the assumptions and predictions of the various sexual selection models, refer to the table provided on the next page (statements in quotes are cited directly from the paper).

3. Sensory bias models of sexual selection examine the origins of female preference, not their subsequent evolution. Outline a system in which sensory bias establishes a preference, but direct selection or good genes models lead to the female preference evolving.

Sensory bias models of sexual selection propose that the preference for any given male trait evolved *before* the male trait itself. Because sensory bias models require female preferences to predate male traits, phylogenetic analyses—those that examine the evolutionary relationships between different species—are paramount, as was emphasized in the swordtail and frog examples provided in the text. In contrast, indirect selection models such as Fisher's runaway model or the good genes model propose that the male trait and the female preference for the male trait co-evolve due, for instance, to some form of genetic linkage (Ryan, 1997). Nevertheless, it is possible for several forces (sensory bias and indirect

ASSUMPTIONS	DIRECT SELECTION	INDIRECT SELECTION: RUNAWAY HYPOTHESIS	INDIRECT SELECTION: PARASITE HYPOTHESIS
Female fitness is affected directly by her preference.	√	Females exerting particular preferences may enjoy *indirect* fitness benefits.	Female fitness is affected indirectly by her preference (e.g., improved genetic constitution of her offspring—resistance genes).
Equilibrium conditions can be achieved.	√	Equilibrium cannot be achieved as long as female preferences evolve more rapidly than the male trait.	Equilibrium cannot be achieved as long as genes for parasite resistance are constantly changing (e.g., if parasite evolution mandates changes in resistance genes).
Genetic correlations can lead to exaggeration of the trait and preference.	No genetic correlations are necessary.	√	√
"Established preferences are arbitrary with respect to male survival."		√	Females choose males that have a higher probability of survival due to parasite resistance.
Heritable variation exists in the male trait.		√	√

PREDICTIONS	DIRECT SELECTION	INDIRECT SELECTION: RUNAWAY HYPOTHESIS	INDIRECT SELECTION: PARASITE HYPOTHESIS*
A correlation exists between female mating preference and female fitness.	√	√	√
Correlations exist between the *strength* of the female preference and male phenotype (i.e., preference and traits co-evolve).		√	√
Exaggerated traits promote male attractiveness at the expense of survival.		√	
The trait in question should be heritable.		√	√
Females prefer males with more highly exaggerated traits.		√	√

*From a comparative perspective, the parasite hypothesis also predicts that species exposed to more parasites should exhibit more exaggerated traits (e.g., if genetic correlations promote more extreme forms of parasite resistance in such species *and* if male traits such as plumage coloration indicate the degree of parasitism). Furthermore, the parasite hypothesis predicts increases in parasite resistance over time.

selection) to act upon the establishment and persistence of female choice, and we will focus on this interaction.

To answer the question at hand, imagine a set of species in which the auditory system is tuned to low frequencies and that this "tuning" is the result of selection pressures favoring detection of prey items that emit low frequency sounds. In a more recently evolved lineage, you discover that males who emit lower frequency sounds are more appealing to females. But in more primitive lineages, males do not use low frequency sounds to attract females (the male trait is absent in these species). Thus, it is possible that males in the recent lineage have exploited the sensory biases of females for their own benefit. That is, males have taken advantage of the fact that low frequency sounds are attractive to females in the context of prey detection. In this situation, female preferences for males that emit low frequency sounds *arose* because males exploited the sensory systems of females. Support for this hypothesis could be obtained by traveling into the phylogenetic past and asking whether females of extant, but more primitive, lineages (whose auditory systems are tuned in similar ways) also prefer males that produce low frequency calls, even though the males in those populations do not exhibit such a trait!

Now that we understand how the male trait arose, we can ask questions regarding the persistence of this male trait in the population. Let's assume that only large males can produce low frequency calls and that large males are healthier than small males. As a consequence, females that choose large males that emit low frequency vocalizations may receive indirect benefits in the form of **good genes**. Over time, the genes coding the female preference for low frequency sound and the genes coding for males that exhibit such a trait become linked—that is, the gene for the preference and the trait are passed on to all offspring, but only the appropriate gene is expressed depending on the sex of the offspring. Genetic linkages could account for the persistence of the male trait and the female preference for this trait; to examine the potential for co-evolution, we could assess whether a positive correlation exists between the strength of the female preference and the frequency of male mating vocalizations.

In summary, female preferences for low frequency sound arose through direct selection but in a context unrelated to mate choice (i.e., prey detection). Males exploited this preexisting preference by generating low frequency mating vocalizations. Thus, female preferences for this male trait arose due to sensory exploitation. The persistence of the male trait, which may be indicative of the indirect benefits a female will receive, could be attributed to runaway or good genes processes, whereby the genes for the male trait and the female preference become linked over time.

4. Why do you suppose it is so difficult to demonstrate mate-choice copying? Pick a species of your choice and design an experiment that would examine whether mate-choice copying is present. How many controls did you need to construct to rule out alternative hypotheses to mate-choice copying?

Mate-choice copying refers to a situation in which females that are not directly involved in a courtship interaction but that observe the choice of the watched female end up choosing males that were previously chosen. In this sense, the current mating success of males depends on past mating success, such that males that were chosen previously have a higher probability of being chosen by different females in the future. Also, the mate-choice decisions of the female depend not only on intrinsic mating preferences but also on mating events that occur within their social group (events that are within range for the observer female to detect). Of course, above and beyond mate-choice copying, there are many potential reasons why a female might exhibit a preference for previously chosen males. Given the number of plausible alternatives (see below), it is often difficult to pinpoint mate-choice copying as the force underlying female preferences.

The vast majority of mate-choice copying studies have been conducted in fish. Because the protocols for investigating this phenomenon in fish are well established, let's choose green swordtail fish (*Xiphophorus helleri*) as our study organism (ambitious students are urged to breach the status quo and test these ideas in different taxa!). The first step to establishing that mate-choice copying exists is to determine whether swordtail females base their future mate-choice decisions on the decisions made by other females in the population. To test this, we would need four swordtails per trial—two males and two females. The two males would be placed at opposite sides of a small aquarium, a model female would be placed near one of the two males, and a focal female would be allowed to observe the fabricated mate-choice decision of the model female. The second step to this experiment involves determining whether the focal female prefers the male that the model female was observed to choose. For this part of the investigation, we would remove the model female and allow the focal female to choose between the two males. If, in a significant proportion of the trials, the model female prefers the male that was previously chosen, then our results would be consistent with the hypothesis that swordtail females copy the mate-choice decisions of others. To be convinced that this is the case, however, we would have to conduct a series of controls. What other factors could be involved in these apparent events of mate-choice copying?

Following the lead of one of the most controlled studies on mate-choice copying to date (Dugatkin, 1992), the following alternative hypotheses would need to be ruled out:

a. *Both swordtail females choose the same male independently.* Switching the position of the model female across trials could test this hypothesis.

b. *Because swordtail fish are a social species, females could be drawn to the area of the experimental tank that most recently had the largest group of fish (schooling hypothesis).* If this hypothesis were true, then we would expect the focal females to prefer the side of the tank that most recently had the largest group of fish, *regardless of sex*. Thus, we could replace the males from the initial experiment with females to see whether the same results were obtained.

c. *Females prefer areas that had been recently occupied by a male and a female, regardless of whether the male was courting.* Here we could minimize the courtship behavior of males by blocking their view of the model female (while still allowing both the model and focal females to see the male) and proceed with a similar procedure as described in the initial experiment.

d. *Swordtail females are attracted to males that exhibit behavior indicative of previous mating experience (e.g., increased activity).* To investigate this hypothesis, we could conduct the first half of our initial experiment wherein the focal female watches the mate-choice decision of the model, but in the second part of the experiment we could replace the model female with a naive female. Here, we could assess whether females have a penchant for choosing males that display behavior associated with previous courting experience.

e. *Swordtail females remember the side of the tank in which previous courtship interactions occurred but they do not remember previously chosen males.* In this case, we could conduct an experiment in which the position of the two males (chosen and not chosen) is reversed, such that the focal female is exposed to a different arrangement of males in the second half of the trial.

These are only some possible alternatives. As an individual or group exercise, construct several additional hypotheses regarding why females might prefer previously chosen males and, if you wish, design experiments that will allow you to address these alternatives empirically. If all of these alternatives are rejected, then we can be confident that females copy the mate-choice decisions of other females.

5. *Pick any of the numerous dating game shows on television and watch a series of episodes. As you watch, imagine yourself as an ethologist studying mate choice. What sort of traits do males prefer in females? What traits do females prefer in males? Can you say anything about how your observations match up against current models of sexual selection?*

Let's say we have watched several episodes of a dating game show in which females were given the opportunity to choose among a large cohort of males taken at random from the population. The male participants were required to provide information about their experience working with children and their miscellaneous skills as well as supplying a recent photograph. For purposes of argument, imagine that females were significantly more likely to choose (1) males who had culinary skills, (2) males who demonstrated some level of experience working with children, and (3) handsome males. According to sexual selection theory, the first two criteria (culinary skills and experience with children) likely fall under the **direct benefits** category. For instance, males who can cook gourmet meals would certainly provide their date with higher-quality (e.g., nutritive value) food than males who place an "order-for-two" at the nearest fast food restaurant. However, caution should be used in interpreting the underlying reasons for this choice. It could very well be that culinary specialists earn a higher income than males that rely on fast food (ingredients for gourmet dishes may be more expensive than the typical fast food meal). Thus, the female's choice for males that are well versed in the culinary arts may be confounded by income, which also constitutes a potential direct benefit for the female (how would you disentangle these two aspects of female choice?). Previous work with children might indicate to the female that a male is dedicated to parental duties and thus would provide the care necessary to raise viable offspring. This too constitutes a direct benefit to the female in terms of increasing progeny number or enhancing offspring survival. Now, let's focus on the females' choice of handsome males. Some studies have demonstrated a correlation between attractiveness and facial symmetry in humans, with more symmetrical individuals deemed more attractive (Grammer and Thornhill, 1994; but see Swaddle and Cuthill, 1995). Although the role of facial symmetry in human female mate choice remains disputable, let us assume for purposes of argument that symmetry is attractive and that symmetry indicates something about the quality of a male's genetic makeup. If this is the case, then the females who choose handsome males may receive **indirect benefits** in the form of quality genes being contributed to their offspring. Thus, this particular aspect of female mate choice falls under the scope of good genes models of sexual selection.

MULTIPLE-CHOICE QUESTIONS

1. Sexual imprinting occurs when
   a. juveniles copy the mate-choice decisions of same-sex adults.
   b. young animals learn what constitutes an appropriate mate from observing adults in their population.
   c. young animals are taught actively by adults to prefer certain traits in individuals of the opposite sex.
   d. males learn which types of nuptial gifts are attractive to females through trial and error.
   e. the development of mate-choice preferences is shaped by genotype alone.

2. Which of the following examples is inconsistent with direct benefits received by females via mate choice?
   a. Females choose males that establish nests that provide safe haven.
   b. Females choose males that provide large nuptial gifts.
   c. Females prefer males that demonstrate superior foraging abilities.

    d. Females choose males with low levels of fluctuating asymmetry.

    e. Females prefer males that are better able to deter neighboring males that may harass the female.

3. Intersexual selection is to intrasexual selection as
    a. mate-choice copying is to runaway selection.
    b. male-male combat is to sensory exploitation.
    c. female mate choice is to male-male combat.
    d. handicap principle is to female mate choice.
    e. good genes models are to sensory exploitation.

4. Zahavi's handicap hypothesis suggests that females
    a. use traits that are honest indicators of male quality when choosing mates.
    b. choose males based on the extent to which direct benefits are received.
    c. do not benefit (directly or indirectly) from making mate-choice decisions.
    d. dismiss males that demonstrate the ability to survive with elaborate traits.
    e. base their mate-choice decisions on a male's ability to attract other females.

5. Which of the following is *not* associated with sensory exploitation hypotheses of female mate choice?
    a. phylogenetic analyses
    b. hypothesis regarding the origin of female mate choice
    c. in an evolutionary sense, males "take advantage of" preexisting sensory biases of females
    d. the long-term maintenance of female mate choice
    e. transmission of sensory traits across generations via social learning

6. Cross-fostering experiments are *most* useful for examining
    a. how behavior is shaped by the environment an animal inhabits early in life.
    b. how certain genetic crosses influence behavior.
    c. the effects of specific genes on the development of behavior patterns.
    d. the evolutionary history of female mate choice.
    e. the relative effects of male-male competition and female mate choice in the process of sexual selection.

7. Which of the following statements regarding runaway sexual selection models is *false*?
    a. Two genes exist—one gene that codes for the male trait and one gene that codes for the female preference—but only one gene is expressed in each sex.
    b. Runaway selection can promote increasingly exaggerated male traits and female preferences.
    c. Two genetically derived traits cannot co-evolve.

d. There is genetic linkage of the alleles that code for the male trait and the female preference.

e. There is positive correlation between the strength of the female preference and the male phenotype.

8. The Hamilton-Zuk parasite resistance hypothesis falls under which category of sexual selection models?
   a. direct benefits
   b. sensory exploitation
   c. good genes
   d. runaway selection
   e. none of the above

9. Which of the following statements does *not* apply to Höglund and colleagues' studies on mate-choice copying in black grouse?
   a. Females synchronize their trips to male territories.
   b. Females copy the choices of other females only when the courting male has superior qualities.
   c. Stuffed "dummy" females were constructed to assess whether females prefer males that had mated previously.
   d. Younger, inexperienced females show a greater propensity to engage in mate-choice copying than older, experienced females.
   e. A single male grouse monopolizes mating opportunity on the lek.

10. Fluctuating asymmetry refers to
    a. asymmetrical traits that confer a fitness advantage in the form of increased reproductive success.
    b. random deviations from perfect symmetry of the body on its right and left sides of the body.
    c. deviations from perfect symmetry that fluctuate from the right to the left sides of the body throughout an organism's lifetime.
    d. any trait that indicates the overall health of an individual.
    e. deviations from perfect symmetry that result from an extremely stable environment during development.

REVIEW AND CHALLENGE QUESTIONS

1. Apart from differential investment in gametes, what other factors might be involved in females being the choosier of the two sexes? Under what circumstances should males be choosy as well?

2. Describe at least three major components to the runaway sexual selection hypothesis. Also, contrast how runaway sexual selection might work when female preferences are determined genetically versus culturally.

3. Obtain a copy of a recent review by Birkhead and Pizzari (2002) entitled "Postcopulatory sexual selection" (*Nature Reviews Genetics*, vol. 3, p. 262–273). Drawing on the concepts outlined in this paper, discuss how both male-male competition and female mate choice could be involved in the process of sexual selection *after* insemination has occurred.

4. Exaggerated male traits are sometimes described as being the result of an elegant balance between natural and sexual selection. Indeed, Ryan (1997) stated that ". . . the male trait evolves to some compromise between the different optima favored by natural and sexual selection. . . ."Based on what you have learned in this chapter, why do you think exaggerated male traits are described as such?

5. Imagine a situation in which some males in a population mimic the behavior of females. For instance, in tiger salamanders, some males (M1) will mimic the "tail-nudging" behavior of a female and cause an unsuspecting male (M2) to deposit a spermatophore (i.e., a packet of sperm). M1 then deposits his own spermatophore on top of that of M2. Thus, a female will pick up the sperm of the mimic instead of the sperm from the original courting male. How would you classify this type of behavior—as intrasexual or intersexual selection? Why?

ANSWER KEY FOR MULTIPLE-CHOICE QUESTIONS

1.	b	6.	a
2.	d	7.	c
3.	c	8.	c
4.	a	9.	b
5.	d	10.	b

CHAPTER 7 | Mating Systems

Discussion Questions

1. Define and distinguish among serial monogamy, serial polygyny, simultaneous polygyny, promiscuity with pair bonds, and promiscuity without pair bonds.

Understanding the differences between mating systems and the selection pressures and environmental gradients that shape mating patterns is essential for analyses of reproductive behavior, intrasexual and intersexual selection, and for examining the relative fitness of individuals within a population. In the above question, you are asked to define and differentiate between five types of mating systems:

Serial monogamy. Males *and* females maintain the same mating partner for an entire breeding season.

Serial (sequential) polygyny. Males establish short-term pair bonds with many females during one breeding season; these pair bonds are established sequentially—that is, males mate with only one female at any given time, but over the entire breeding season males pair with multiple females.

Simultaneous polygyny. Males have access to (and mate with) multiple females at any given time during the breeding season.

Promiscuity without pair bonds. Males *and* females mate with multiple partners during the breeding season without establishing pair bonds; neither males nor females mate exclusively with certain partners.

Promiscuity with pair bonds (polygynandry). Several females form pair bonds with several males simultaneously, and multiple males jointly defend the territories of multiple females.

The chief differences between these mating systems can be cast in terms of (1) the number of partners that individuals of either sex obtain, and (2) the time frame over which the partnerships occur. In serial monogamous and promiscuous systems, males and females adhere to similar mating policies (excluding EPCs—see Discussion Question 4) in that both sexes associate with either one or multiple mates during the breeding season. In serial monogamous systems, both sexes mate with only *one* partner during the entire breeding season, while in serial promiscuous systems, both sexes mate with *multiple* partners during the breeding season. Furthermore, in serial monogamous and polygynandrous systems, pair bonds are established for the duration of the breeding season—that is, there is some form of mating exclusivity. Promiscuous systems without pair bonds, however, are characterized by the lack of mating exclusivity because at no time during the breeding season does either sex establish a lasting bond with one or even several members of the opposite sex. In polygynous mating systems, males and females often adhere to different mating policies. For instance, males may mate with several females during the breeding season, while females may mate with only one male (again, excluding EPCs). The primary difference between serial (sequential) and simultaneous polygyny is the time frame over which males distribute their mating efforts among many females. In serial polygynous systems, males dedicate their time to *one* female for short periods, but establish many of these bonds throughout the breeding season. Conversely, in simultaneous polygynous systems, males dedicate their mating efforts to *many* females for the duration of the breeding season.

2. Read Jenni and Collier's 1972 article, "Polyandry in the American jacana (Jacana spinosa), in Auk *(vol. 89, pp. 743–765). What selective forces favored polyandry in jacanas, and how did ecological factors affect selection pressure?*

The mating system of the American jacana, as described by Jenni and Collier, fits nicely within the definition of **resource defense polyandry** proposed in this chapter. Specifically, female American jacanas defend large territories that include the small territories of many males.

Several key factors favor resource defense polyandry in the jacanas. Although the following list of factors is not exhaustive, it is instructive with respect to understanding polyandry in American jacanas.

a. *Female territorial defense.* A female American jacana defends not only her own territory but also the territories of the two to three males that reside within her "superterritory." Female jacanas are capable of defending more spacious territories than their male partners, presumably because they are much larger (in fact, almost twice as large as males) and thus competitively superior when it comes to territorial defense.

b. *Male parental care.* If females invest substantial amounts of energy defending their own territory and the territories of several males, reduced investment in the offspring might be expected. Thus, the bulk of offspring care falls on the shoulders of the males. Indeed, female jacanas provide little (or no) parental care, while males establish nesting sites, incubate, brood, attend, and defend the young.

Note: Taken together, factors a and b constitute **sex role reversal** in the jacanas.

c. *Long breeding seasons.* When breeding seasons are long, territorial males have the opportunity to sire multiple clutches of eggs in one season, despite the fact that females partition their reproductive investment among many males. Long breeding seasons may reduce the "conflict of interest" between the sexes (see the "Dunnocks" section of this chapter). Jacanas inhabit tropical marsh habitats and breed essentially year round.

d. *Limited resources and parent-offspring competition.* When food resources are limited, mechanisms that reduce competition between adults and their offspring should be favored. Jenni and Collier suggest that food resources for the young are critical, particularly because females produce relatively small eggs that may not provide adequate food reserves to sustain the young after hatching; reduced investment in each egg allows females to accommodate egg demand—that is, to trade egg quality for egg quantity. Polyandrous mating systems facilitate reduced parent-offspring competition by decreasing the density of adults in the breeding area, while maintaining a positive reproductive trajectory for both males and females. To get a better handle on this, imagine a polyandrous system in which the territory of one female encompasses three male territories. Here we have a total of four adults vying for limited resources, likely at the expense of offspring survival. In a monogamous system where all else is equal, we would have six adults (three males and three females) vying for the same ration of resources, which could be of further detriment to the offspring.

Of these four selective forces mediating polyandry in American jacanas, the latter two are obviously influenced by ecological factors. Jacanas inhabit the tropics, where temperature and photoperiod remain relatively constant and only moderate dry seasons occur. These environmental factors are conducive to long breeding seasons which, in turn, favor polyandry. More important, however, jacanas inhabit tropical marsh habitats in which suitable territories—that is, those that provide enough food for the young—are patchily distributed. Food limitation in Jenni and Collier's study site was also exacerbated by the recent destruction of prime jacana habitat (e.g., heterogeneous vegetation). Under such conditions, strong selection pressures may exist for mating systems that reduce parent-offspring competition for food resources; both polygyny and polyandry could theoretically alleviate competitive pressures. Interestingly, though, the relatively high rate of offspring mortality (due to food restriction, predation, and habitat disturbance) coupled with sex role reversal stacks the deck in favor of polyandry. When offspring mortality rates are high, it pays to produce more young, so as to increase the probability that at least a few will survive. Large female jacanas are released from their parental care responsibilities and have access to a larger resource pool than males (e.g., by defending the territories of several males). In turn, the females can invest more resources in producing many eggs, which may enhance the probability of offspring survival. All in all, polyandry and its associated sex role reversal in American jacanas are favored when ecological conditions lead to increased offspring mortality. Increased egg production reduces the risk of having entire clutches die and can be accomplished best if females have access to a substantial resource pool (e.g., defending large territories) and can shunt more of these resources toward the manufacturing of eggs (e.g., by investing less in parental care).

3. Why do you think that polygamous mating systems favor the evolution of more deadly diseases in animals and humans? Think about this from the perspective of the disease-causing agent.

Before we dive into the question at hand, let us briefly examine a day in the life of a virus—one agent of infectious disease. Viruses are invisible packets of nucleic acids, usually ribonucleic acids, that can be transmitted either from mother to offspring (*vertical transmission*) or between individuals via biotic (e.g., insects, humans) or abiotic (e.g., air, water) vectors (*horizontal transmission*). The recent global surge of the SARS (severe acute respiratory syndrome) virus is a testament to how quickly viruses can invade a population and how virulent they can become. **Virulence** essentially refers to the damage quotient or deadliness associated with any particular pathogen; higher virulence is usually associated with faster replication rates in viruses. Viruses usually infect the cells of their host and use their host's molecular machinery to replicate. When enough copies of the virus are made, the cell explodes (lysis), releasing the progeny to facilitate further invasion.

For the sake of argument, imagine that a virus has two options: (1) replicate fast and kill the host, or (2) replicate slow and keep the host around (in reality, these options fall along a continuum). Two major factors might play into the virus' decision of which road to travel: (1) the type of vector that it relies on for transmission, and (2) the transmission rate. If the virus can replicate without harming the vector (e.g., the air or water), then it pays to replicate quickly. But if replication harms the vector (e.g., the humans), the virus may opt to replicate slower. After all, if the host dies, so too does the virus, rendering the fitness of the entire viral population within the dead host zero! With respect to transmission rates, if the virus has a high probability of being transmitted before the host dies, then it should replicate quickly. However, if transmission rates are low, the virus should decrease replication rates, thereby keeping the host around for long enough to ensure transmission.

Based on the above descriptions, we can now tackle the question of why polygamous mating systems might favor the evolution of more virulent diseases in animals. Here we are dealing with a biotic host, thus the pathogen should be selected to replicate at a rate that maximizes progeny number without destroying its victim before being transmitted to another host. Transmission rates may vary between mating systems, particularly for sexually transmitted diseases or for those that are spread via close contact. In monogamous mating systems, individuals usually have one partner, thus the rate of disease transmission is likely to be low. As such, pathogens may benefit from replicating slowly or lying dormant during the nonbreeding seasons, as diseases that kill their host quickly have a miniscule chance of being transmitted in monogamous systems. But in polygamous or promiscuous systems, the odds are weighed in favor of increased virulence. In these mating systems, animals mate multiple times and the probability of transmission is increased dramatically compared to monogamous systems. The pathogen need not worry about killing its host before being transmitted and, in turn, it is selected for high replication rates and high virulence. All in all, the fact that transmission rates are higher in polygamous and promiscuous systems favors selection for more deadly pathogen strains.

The incorporation of evolutionary biology and animal behavior into the study of the incidence, distribution, and control of disease (epidemiology) has gained increasing attention over the past decade (e.g., Ewald, 1993, 2000; Galvani, 2003). In years to come, this integrative approach will likely augment our understanding of virulence and the measures that should be taken to combat deadly disease.

4. Define an EPC. How does this differ from an extrapair mating? Why did it take ethologists so long to recognize the extent of EPCs in nature? How has molecular genetics revolutionized the way we think of mating systems in birds?

EPCs, or **extrapair copulations**, refer to situations where the male and/or female of a socially monogamous pair copulates with individuals other than their pair-bond partner. Extrapair copulations differ from extrapair matings (fertilizations) in the sense that copulations do not necessarily result in fertilization. That is, we cannot make any assumptions about extrapair mating *success* by investigating copulation alone—fertilization is essential for extrapair flings to be successful!

Although it is now well established that extrapair copulations occur and that extrapair fertilizations can contribute significantly to a given clutch, the extent of EPCs was not always recognized. In any given observational experiment, researchers may document only a small proportion of the EPCs that actually occur. Even the most rigorous field study is likely to underestimate both the number of EPCs and their contribution to the clutch due to time limitations, viewing obstructions, and so on. Add the lack of molecular techniques to analyze parentage, and it is easy to see why early studies on mating systems were at a significant disadvantage (in terms of realizing the extent of EPCs) relative to those conducted in the present. Molecular genetics techniques (e.g., electrophoresis, DNA fingerprinting, microsatellites) have significantly enhanced our understanding of mating systems. First, these techniques have allowed ethologists to meticulously and unambiguously assign parentage (i.e., determine the proportion of offspring sired by parental males versus cuckolding males). Second, molecular techniques have fine-tuned our understanding of mating systems. For instance, without such techniques, we might still consider extrapair offspring as a minor blemish on a male's record rather than as a significant force shaping virtually all aspects of intrasexual competition—from male behavior to sperm morphology (see Discussion Question 5). In addition, parentage analyses have been a linchpin in the emergence of the distinction between social and genetic monogamy. For an intriguing account of how genetics can enhance our understanding of organismal systems, refer to Avise (2002).

5. How has natural selection via sperm competition shaped both sperm morphology and male behavior? Also, create a list of potential ways in which females may affect sperm competition and its outcome.

Sperm competition is a less visible form of intrasexual selection than overt male-male fighting. But as described in the text, sperm competition is a powerful postcopulatory mechanism by which males can increase their fitness. Thus, selection should favor sperm that wield the ability to outcompete rival sperm. What kinds of characteristics should selection favor? First, it may be that males with larger ejaculates experience greater fertilization success (as natural selection favors sheer volume), which is likely accomplished by increased testis size. Second, certain sperm characteristics such as increased velocity, endurance, or viability in the female reproductive tract (see "Sperm Competition in Sea Urchins" in the text) and the advent of sperm with a killer streak—that is, those that destroy the sperm of rivals—would certainly be favored by selection. A fascinating example of how sperm competition might influence gamete morphology is the giant sperm of some species of fruit fly (*Drosophila spp.*), which may be twenty times longer than the flies themselves (Pitnick et al., 1995)! A recent study by Miller and Pitnick (2002) postulated that the reproductive tracts of female fruit flies might favor longer, higher-quality sperm. Thus, selection pressures mediated by female reproductive morphology can drive the evolution of sperm morphology. Some materials associated with the sperm (e.g., those produced by accessory glands) may also respond to the pressures of sperm competition. For instance, some studies report that males may utilize substances that prevent rival sperm from entering the female reproductive tract (e.g., sperm plugs or degradative compounds; Jivoff, 1997; Buckland-Nicks, 1998). Lastly, male reproductive morphology may be tuned to the prospects of sperm competition; male damselflies possess "microspinations" on their penes that may aid in the removal of rival sperm from the female reproductive tract (Robinson and

Novak, 1997). With respect to male behavior, sperm competition pressures may favor males with longer copulation durations (enabling them to secure access to the female or transfer more sperm) and more effective mate-guarding tactics.

Recent research suggests that females play a key role in mediating the outcome of sperm competition via some form of cryptic choice (Birkhead, 1998, and related arguments in Eberhard, 2000; Kempenaers et al., 2000; Pitnick and Brown, 2000). Females could promote sperm competition or selectively favor sperm using a host of behavioral, morphological, and physiological mechanisms. For instance, females could eject sperm from low-quality males (subordinates), possess sperm storage organs or mate multiple times to incite rigorous sperm competition, utilize physiologically based recognition mechanisms to determine sperm quality or kinship (e.g., haplotype or major histocompatibility complex recognition; Birkhead and Pizzari, 2002; see references in Chapter 3), or possess reproductive morphologies tailored toward certain sperm types (see fruit fly example above).

MULTIPLE-CHOICE QUESTIONS

1. Insects displaying female defense polygyny exhibit which of the following characteristics?
   a. Females are short-lived.
   b. Females are grouped close together in space.
   c. Females have low fecundity.
   d. Females mate shortly after becoming adults.
   e. all of the above

2. Cooperative polyandry (CP) differs from resource defense polyandry (RDP) in which of the following ways?
   a. In CP many males defend a female's territory, while in RDP females defend superterritories that include the smaller territories of many males.
   b. In CP females mate with one male, while in RDP females mate with many males.
   c. In CP females mate with many males sequentially, while in RDP females mate with many males simultaneously.
   d. In CP males mate with multiple females, while in RDP females mate with multiple males.
   e. In CP males assume all of the parental care duties, while in RDP females perform all of the parental care.

3. When social pair bonding occurs, individuals establish
   a. pair bonds and mate with multiple partners during the breeding season.
   b. exclusive pair bonds and mate with only one partner during the breeding season.

   c. a pair bond with one partner but may mate with multiple partners during the breeding season.

   d. multiple pair bonds in a sequential fashion during the breeding season.

   e. multiple pair bonds during the mating season but mate with only one partner.

4. Which of the following techniques has enhanced our understanding of how extrapair matings translate into extrapair fertilizations?

   a. radioimmunoassay

   b. genetic recombination

   c. truncation selection

   d. DNA fingerprinting

   e. quantitative trait loci mapping

5. In systems where the potential for intense sperm competition exists, selection should *not* favor

   a. sperm with greater velocity and/or endurance.

   b. large testes with greater sperm production.

   c. decreased copulation duration.

   d. specialized sperm morphology.

   e. increased time guarding the female after copulation if last-male precedence exists.

6. In polyandrous mating systems

   a. both females and males have multiple partners during the breeding season.

   b. females mate with more than one male during the breeding season.

   c. females mate only once per breeding season.

   d. males mate with more than one female during the breeding season.

   e. females mate with multiple males every other breeding season.

7. Several males form pair bonds with several females simultaneously in which of the following mating systems:

   a. serial polygamy

   b. polyandry

   c. sequential polygamy

   d. polygynandry

   e. polygyny

8. Which of the following statements regarding Margie Profet's hypothesis on menstruation is *false?*

   a. There is a link between promiscuous breeding systems and female reproductive health.

   b. Menstruation should be least common in breeding systems where females engage in sexual activity with many partners.

   c. Sperm are vectors of disease.

   d. Promiscuous mating systems might expose females to greater quantities and diversity of sperm.

   e. Menstruation is a defense against pathogens carried by sperm.

9. Which statement does *not* follow from the polygyny threshold model?

   a. Polygyny should occur in patchy environments where males can defend valuable resources.

   b. Moving between territories could decrease reproductive success if all other females stay put.

   c. A female's decision to occupy a certain territory depends on the number of females already present but not on territory quality.

   d. The quality of a male's territory should affect his mating success.

   e. When females settle onto territories at the same time, those on monogamous and polygamous territories should have approximately equal fitness.

10. Which of the following statements about breeding systems is *true*?

   a. Genetic analyses of parentage have not furthered our understanding of mating systems.

   b. Mating systems are classified solely on the basis of pair-bond formation.

   c. Within a species, only one type of mating system can evolve.

   d. The occurrence of extrapair copulations has led ethologists to consider the difference between social and genetic monogamy.

   e. All human populations adhere to strict monogamy—that is, both social monogamy and genetic monogamy.

REVIEW AND CHALLENGE QUESTIONS

1. As described in the chapter, extrapair copulations (EPCs) are widespread and, in many cases, the cuckolded male experiences dramatic decreases in fertilization success (and thus, fitness). Because extrapair copulations pose such imminent risks, one might expect males to adopt tactics that minimize the possibility of cuckoldry. Construct at least two hypotheses regarding how males could reduce the probability of EPCs.

2. Describe in detail the assumptions and predictions of the polygyny threshold model and its implications for the distribution of females in a population. Also, keep the polygyny threshold model in mind as you read Chapter 13, in which the concept of ideal free distributions is presented. What characteristics do the polygyny threshold model and the ideal free distribution model share? What sets these two models apart?

3. Electrophoresis was introduced as a technique used to determine parentage and/or the frequency of successful, but unfaithful copulations. Peruse the cur-

rent literature and describe at least one additional "cutting-edge" technique that has emerged as a powerful way to examine parentage.

4. Why is it important to make the distinction between social monogamy and genetic monogamy?

5. Why do you suppose that kamikaze sperm would evolve? Propose at least one hypothetical mechanism by which these killer sperm might be capable of selectively eliminating the sperm of other males (i.e., killing foreign sperm without destroying sperm derived from their same ejaculate).

ANSWER KEY FOR MULTIPLE-CHOICE QUESTIONS

1.	e	6.	b
2.	a	7.	d
3.	c	8.	b
4.	d	9.	c
5.	c	10.	d

CHAPTER 8 | Kinship

DISCUSSION QUESTIONS

1. Why would it be an advantage for animals to gauge very small differences in blood kinship relationships? Why, for example, would it often be better if animals could distinguish relatives at the level of cousins (r = 0.125) rather than simply distinguishing siblings (r = 0.5)? What sorts of benefits might be possible when small differences in relatedness could be gauged?

What could be the potential advantages of fine-tuning **kin recognition** mechanisms to the level of cousins? The simple answer to this question is that if recognition mechanisms can accurately discriminate to the level of cousins, animals endowed with such recognition abilities may experience inclusive fitness and/or individual fitness benefits. According to Sherman and his colleagues (1997), kin recognition is "differential treatment of conspecifics differing in genetic relatedness." These authors outline several hypothesized benefits to kin recognition, the first of which centers on nepotistic behavior. If an animal is capable of accurately distinguishing siblings from nonkin, and the costs of helping siblings are relatively low, then in terms of **inclusive fitness** it may benefit this animal to aid its siblings (e.g., alarm calling, coalition formation). If the animal is capable of recognizing both siblings ($r = 0.50$) and cousins ($r = 0.125$) and the costs of helping are especially low, then the animal can boost its inclusive fitness even further by providing aid to sibs and more distantly related cousins. Sherman and his colleagues also propose that kin recognition could reduce inbreeding depression (or "optimize the balance between inbreeding and outbreeding"), which would presumably improve individual fitness. Inbreeding depression is a phenomenon whereby matings between closely related individuals yield less viable (or less competitive) offspring than matings between nonkin. If an animal is capable of distinguishing only siblings, then cousins would be treated the same as nonkin and, as a result, some level of inbreeding with closely related kin ($r = 0.125$) might occur. In contrast, if an animal treats both siblings and cousins as kin and avoids mating with these individuals, then the probability of siring inbred, inferior offspring is reduced. Although inbreeding may compromise the fitness of one's offspring, even when cousins mate (Meagher et al., 2000; Eklund, 1996), the level of fine-tuning of the kin recognition mechanisms may depend both on the overall fitness costs and benefits of mating with close or more distantly related kin and on the balance between acceptance and rejection errors (e.g., if the kin recognition mechanism is too stringent, the probability of rejecting nonkin mating partners may increase; Sherman et al., 1997).

2. *Read Emlen's 1995 article "An evolutionary theory of the family," in* Proceedings of the National Academy of Sciences, U.S.A. *(vol. 92, pp. 8092–8099). List the evidence for and against three of the predictions that we did not examine in this chapter.*

Emlen's seminal review meshed kin selection, reproductive skew theory, and ecological constraints theory to generate fifteen predictions about family dynamics. Here, we will focus on Predictions 5, 10, and 15, which fall under three of Emlen's four subheadings—Kinship and cooperation, Disruption after breeder loss or replacement, and Reproductive sharing leads to extended families, respectively; both predictions of the fourth subheading (The importance of delayed dispersal) were covered in the chapter.

Prediction 5: Sexually related aggression will be less prevalent in family groups than in otherwise comparable groups composed of nonrelatives. This is because opposite-sex close genetic relatives will avoid incestuously mating with one another. As was alluded to in the answer to Discussion Question 1 (above), inbreeding can have deleterious consequences in terms of offspring viability and, as stated by Emlen, promotes homozygosity and the expression of potentially detrimental recessive alleles. Any mechanism that stifles inbreeding should thus be favored. Sexually related aggression can include competitive interactions among males for access to females, competition among females for access to males, and intersexual mating aggression. If inbreeding constitutes a substandard mating strategy, then we might expect relatives to engage in less sexually related aggression than nonrelatives (for example, sons competing with fathers for access to mothers) so as to avoid inbreeding. Emlen indicates that incestuous matings are exceedingly rare in avian and mammalian taxa. But his data also suggest that severe ecological conditions that limit the opportunity to breed outside one's family group may, in fact, lead to incestuous relations.

Prediction 10: Nonreproductive family members will reduce their investment in future offspring after the replacement of a closely related breeder by a more distantly related or unrelated individual.

This prediction is essentially the flip side of Prediction 9, which states that step-parents should invest less in the offspring sired by others than in their own offspring. Prediction 10, however, examines the situation from the perspective of offspring faced with the decision of whether to invest in future young sired by a nonbiological parent. Offspring sired by a replacement parent will be less related to existing nonreproductive individuals than offspring sired by the same set of parents (specifically, one-half as related). According to kin selection theory, the investment provided by existing nonreproductive individuals should be a function of their relatedness to future offspring and the potential inclusive fitness benefits. Investment in future offspring should decrease if the offspring are the product of a replacement father/mother mating with a biological parent. Nonetheless, Emlen indicates that data regarding this prediction are sparse, and for every study providing supporting evidence, there is also a study providing contrary evidence.

Prediction 15: Reproduction will be shared most with those family members to whom the dominant breeders are least closely related. In species in which dominants actively suppress reproduction by subordinates, such suppression will be greatest in those subordinates to whom the dominant is most closely related. Intuitively, one might think that dominants would reproductively suppress individuals who are less closely related. After all, why should an individual stop its closest kin from reproducing? As a clear example of how intuition can contradict reality, Emlen proposes the exact opposite! Why? If the inclusive fitness benefits of staying on the natal territory are high, then an individual has more incentive to stay and is less likely to leave on its own volition (especially if independent breeding opportunities are scant). In contrast, if the inclusive fitness benefits of staying on the natal territory are low (or absent), then an individual has less incentive to stay (especially if independent breeding opportunities are available). But if dominant breeders can provide additional incentives, individuals that are less closely related to the offspring (or dominant breeder) may opt to stay and help. "Staying incentives" may come in the form of reproductive allowance. Essentially, dominant breeders allow distantly related or unrelated subordinates some degree of reproductive opportunity to compensate for the negligible inclusive fitness benefits they gain by staying. Of all of the predictions, this is probably one of the best tested. Supporting evidence exists from groups of lions, white-fronted bee-eaters, dunnocks, and dwarf mongooses.

Given that Emlen's review was published in 1995, there are likely to be a few, if not many, recent empirical studies that address some of these predictions. In fact, there have been at least a dozen new theoretical treatments of this topic since the mid-1990s. As an individual or group exercise, peruse the literature on family dynamics (searching for keywords such as *reproductive skew, dispersal, co-operative breeding, kinship,* and so on), and discuss some supporting or contradictory empirical evidence for Emlen's predictions, as well as any novel theoretical developments in this area.

3. *Try and find some statistics on the rate of child abuse in families where children are adopted. What might you expect based on the logic adopted by Daly and Wilson? What do your data show?*

This question is geared toward testing both your skills as an evolutionary detective and your understanding of Daly and Wilson's predictions regarding relatedness and the incidence of child abuse in human families (see the "Family Dynamics, Prediction 9" section of the text). Although this evolutionary investigation falls in your hands, we can discuss what predictions might arise by examining adoption and family dynamics from an ultimate perspective. Daly and Wilson (1988, 1996) provide evidence that parents are more likely to abuse and kill stepchildren than biological children. We can use kinship theory to explain why such distressing trends emerge. As relatedness coefficients decrease, the inclusive fitness benefits gained by investing in offspring also decrease. When the relatedness coefficient is zero (as in the case of step-parents), investing in unrelated children may constitute a considerable cost without an iota of associated inclusive fitness benefits. As described in the chapter, this asymmetry in the costs and benefits of caring for unrelated children could explain the high incidence of abuse, and even infanticide, in human populations. Now, let us turn to adoption and discuss two potential alternatives. First, let's concentrate on kinship theory and the relatedness coefficient. The parents (nonbiological) of adopted children are, in a substantial portion of cases, unrelated to the child. Cases of adoption differ from stepfamilies in that *both*, rather than one, of the parents are unrelated to the child. In line with Daly and Wilson's logic, relatedness coefficients of zero may spur an increase in child abuse (or infanticide). Because neither parent shares genes with the child in adoption-based families, we might expect adopted children to experience even harsher family circumstances than stepchildren. This logic may be flawed, however, because we have failed to consider the contextual aspects of adoption. Despite both parents being unrelated to the adopted child, there is often some form of mutual agreement to go through with the adoption process; step-parents, however, rarely have a say in family-related events (e.g., pregnancy) that occurred prior to his/her becoming the step-parent. Furthermore, human adoption often occurs when a male and a female are biologically incapable of producing children of their own. In such cases, the fitness of both the male and female is undeniably zero because genetic inheritance cannot occur! However, one could argue that cultural inheritance is an important factor in adoption-based families—that is, with bleak fitness prospects, couples may make the best of a bad situation by settling for passing cultural traits on to young, unrelated individuals. These two contextual aspects of adoption (mutual agreement and "best of a bad situation") may promote harmonious relationships between an adopted child and his/her nonbiological parents in lieu of a family dynamic ridden with abuse. It should be stressed that the latter half of this answer is based purely on speculation and would need to be subject to rigorous socioevolutionary testing before being confirmed as a viable alternative to Daly and Wilson's hypotheses.

4. Based on the parent-offspring conflict model, what differences in weaning behavior would you expect to see between younger and older mammalian mothers?

The **parent-offspring conflict** model predicts that young individuals demand more from their parents than the parents are willing to concede. For both of the parties involved, conflict arises due to asymmetries in relatedness. Each individual has a coefficient of relatedness (r) equal to 1 for "self"—that is, you can't be less than 100 percent related to yourself! However, the relatedness coefficient between parents and offspring in diploid genetic systems is 0.5. Thus, offspring should be more interested in obtaining benefits for themselves than in reducing the demands they place on their parents ($r_{self} > r_{parent}$). Similarly, parents should be more interested in preserving their own potential for future reproductive investment than in investing their entire resource pool in current offspring. In the "Parent-induced Infanticide in Humans" section of the chapter, you were introduced to one scenario where parents may opt to invest less in their offspring to preserve future reproductive opportunity. Young individuals with high potential for future reproduction may be more likely to let current offspring perish (e.g., because of low resource availability) than older individuals with low potential for future reproduction. This same logic can be applied to weaning behavior. Weaning refers to the time at which young become independent of mother's milk as the primary source of nourishment. From the offspring's perspective, it pays to continue feeding on mother's milk for as long as possible. From the mother's perspective, it pays to discontinue feeding current young so as to begin investing in future offspring (e.g., if females can only become sexually receptive *after* weaning). But the balance between the demands of offspring and mother may depend on the mother's potential for future reproductive opportunity. For young mothers with high future reproductive potential, the best strategy may be to discontinue offspring feeding prematurely (or at least on time) in order to accommodate prospective mating opportunities and to begin investing in future young. For older mothers with low future reproductive potential, however, the best strategy may be to invest as much as possible in current young (e.g., provide milk for prolonged periods of time). After all, when prospects of bearing future young are grim, it might pay to invest heavily in current offspring (sometimes even at the expense of one's own survival!). One critical take-home message of this question should be that investment in an offspring depends on the balance between the interests of the offspring and the interests of the parent. As the value of current offspring increases (or the value of future offspring decreases), the balance should be tipped in favor of the offspring's interests. This translates into the offspring enjoying longer periods of nourishment from mother's milk and greater latencies to weaning.

5. How might both kin selection and kin recognition rules be useful in understanding cases of "adoption" in animals?

Adoption in animals, human and nonhuman, refers to caring for offspring that are not one's own in the absence of the offspring's biological parents. From an evolutionary perspective, it may seem disadvantageous to dedicate precious time and energy to caring for somebody else's offspring. However, both kin selection and kin recognition rules may help to shed light on why adoption occurs. As an example of kin selection and adoption, let's examine the social dynamics of common gulls. Bukacinski and his colleagues (2000) examined the social structure of common gull colonies and found that genetic similarity decreased as a function of the distance between nests—that is, the closer the nests, the more related the individuals occupying these nests are likely to be. Adoptions were also more likely to occur among neighbors. Furthermore, neighboring males and females were more closely related to adopted chicks than nonneighboring males and females. These results suggest that relatedness plays a large role in the frequency of adoption in common gulls. More precisely, adoption among neighbors occurs presumably because the inclusive fitness benefits obtained by caring for foster chicks outweigh the costs of investing in additional young. Adoption of a neighbor's offspring should occur more frequently than adoption of nonneighboring offspring because there is a high probability that neighboring chicks are close kin, thus keeping these chicks alive may constitute a considerable inclusive fitness benefit.

How would we interpret similar adoption results in the absence of close kinship? In these instances, we might revisit our kin recognition rules for some insight. As described in this chapter, kin recognition can be accomplished via matching rules (e.g., determining genetic similarity of others using, for instance, specific genetic or chemical cues) or rules of thumb (e.g., if an individual lives nearby, it must be kin). Brown (1998) conducted a study on another species of gull, ring-billed gulls, and found that, despite low levels of relatedness between chicks and foster parents, adoption still occurred at a relatively high frequency within the colony. Even more perplexing, Brown discovered that foster parents raise fewer of their own young than parents that did not adopt. Why would adoption occur in the absence of prospective increases in inclusive fitness? According to Brown, the answer to this question lies in understanding the trade-off between having stringent kin recognition mechanisms and committing kin recognition errors (see also Sherman et al., 1997). The more exclusive a kin recognition rule becomes, the more likely an individual is to erroneously reject close kin, especially if there is a fair bit of variation in genetic, chemical, or site-based cues indicative of relatedness. If the costs of rejecting close kin are high (as they probably are), then relaxing kin recognition rules might be the best strategy. But this opens the door for mistaken nepotism aimed at unrelated individuals—that is, relaxing kin recognition mechanisms increases the probability of making erroneous decisions. This appears to be the case in ring-billed gulls. Brown hypothesized that, because the costs of rejecting kin are especially high (e.g., parental infanticide), it pays to have kin recognition mechanisms that prevent the rejection of close kin, even if this means the occasional acceptance of nonkin (e.g., adoption).

As a further exercise in critical thinking, imagine that you have ruled out kin selection and kin recognition tradeoffs as viable explanations for adoption in your animal system. Where would you turn next? For the sake of entertaining alternative, ultimate hypotheses for adoption in animals, refer to the work of Wisenden and colleagues on brood adoption in convict cichlid fishes (Fraser et al., 1993; Wisenden and Keenleyside, 1992, 1994; Wisenden, 1999).

MULTIPLE-CHOICE QUESTIONS

1. The coefficient of relatedness (r) calculates
    a. the absolute number of genes shared by any two individuals.
    b. differences in the proportion of genes shared by siblings versus cousins.
    c. the probability that any two individuals share genes that are identical by descent.
    d. the likelihood that certain offspring were sired by a particular male.
    e. the overall contribution of kinship to the emergence of certain behavioral patterns.

2. Jerram Brown's "offspring rule" provided a means by which to estimate
    a. fitness benefits and costs of assisting kin.
    b. probability of successfully helping kin.
    c. relatedness.
    d. future expected reproductive success.
    e. parameters associated with kin recognition rules.

3. Haplodiploid genetic systems have which of the following characteristics?
    a. Females are diploid; males are haploid.
    b. Sisters and brothers are related to one another by an average coefficient of relatedness of $r = 0.375$.
    c. Only the queen is diploid; worker females and males are haploid.
    d. Sisters are related to one another by an average coefficient of relatedness of $r = 0.75$.
    e. a and d

4. Hamilton's rule states that a gene that codes for assisting others will increase in frequency when:

    a. $\left[\sum_{i}^{A} rb \right] + c > 0$

b. $\left[\sum_1^A rc\right] + b > 0$

c. $\left[\sum_1^A rb\right] - c < 0$

d. $\left[\sum_1^A rb\right] - c > 0$

e. $\left[\sum_1^A r\right] - bc < 0$

5. The building blocks for Emlen's predictions of family dynamics are
   a. ecological constraints theory, Mendelian genetics, and kin recognition theory.
   b. kin selection theory, ecological constraints theory, and reproductive skew theory.
   c. sexual selection theory, natural selection theory, and kin selection theory.
   d. reproductive skew theory, kin recognition theory, and runaway selection theory.
   e. natural selection theory, individual learning, and cultural transmission.

6. If sex ratio is controlled by female workers in a social insect nest, then the sex ratio should approach:
   a. 3 females: 1 male
   b. 1 female: 2 males
   c. 1 female: 3 males
   d. 2 females: 1 male
   e. 1 female: 1 male

7. Which of the following statements regarding Haig's theory of in-utero parent-offspring conflict is *true*?
   a. Maternal genes should be selected to transfer as many nutrients to the fetus as it requires.
   b. Fetal-derived cells cannot invade the maternal endometrium during implantation.
   c. Hormones produced by the placenta manipulate the in-utero environment in ways that benefit the fetus at a cost to the mother.
   d. Selection will not favor maternal genes that code for resisting invasion of the endometrium by fetal-derived tissues.
   e. Fetal genes should be selected to respect the maternal optimum for nutrient transfer to preserve the mother's future reproductive success.

8. Infanticide will be favored most strongly when a mother's residual reproductive value is

a. low and resources are plentiful.
b. low and resources are scarce.
c. high and resources are plentiful.
d. zero and resources are plentiful.
e. high and resources are scarce.

9. Which of the following statements does *not* relate to sibling rivalry in egret chicks?
   a. Eggs hatch asynchronously.
   b. First-hatched chicks are competitively inferior to second-hatched chicks.
   c. Successful acquisition of a regurgitated food bolus depends on a chick's vertical positioning in the nest.
   d. Age-related dominance hierarchies exist among chicks.
   e. Larger chicks obtain significantly more food than smaller chicks.

10. The conspecific threshold model of kin recognition posits that the evolutionarily stable acceptance threshold is a function of
    a. the fitness consequences of making kin recognition errors (accepting nonkin or rejecting kin).
    b. the relative frequency at which individuals interact with different classes of conspecifics.
    c. simple rules of thumb.
    d. the degree to which interactions between two individuals are amicable.
    e. a and b

REVIEW AND CHALLENGE QUESTIONS

1. As you become more familiar with the literature in behavioral ecology, you will encounter the terms "individual fitness" and "inclusive fitness" with increasing frequency. What is the primary difference between individual and inclusive fitness?

2. Describe the parameters r, b, and c, which make up Hamilton's rule. With respect to each of these parameters, devise a scenario where increased helping behavior might be favored. For instance, think about situations where b and c are held constant but r fluctuates. What types of changes in r might promote helping (conduct the same mental exercise for b and c)?

3. What is the difference between haploid, diploid, and haplodiploid genetic systems? With this difference in mind, describe why females are related to sisters by a coefficient of $r = 0.75$ and to brothers by a coefficient of $r = 0.25$ in haplodiploid systems. Based on what you learned in this chapter, what kinds of consequences could differences in relatedness have for colony dynamics in social insects?

4. In this chapter, you were introduced to optimal skew models as they apply to the partitioning of reproduction amongst members of a group. Obtain a copy of Clutton-Brock's 1998 review of reproductive skew entitled "Reproductive skew, concessions, and limited control" in *Trends in Ecology and Evolution* (vol. 13, pp. 288–292) and Clutton-Brock and his colleagues' 2001 paper entitled "Cooperation, concession, and control in meerkat groups" in *Science* (vol. 291, pp. 478–491). What is the distinction between limited control and optimal models of reproductive skew? How would you test between these two models in cooperatively breeding animals?

5. Develop a scenario for how internal matching templates for kin recognition could be generated by genetic mechanisms, learning, and social learning. Also, based on your readings for Discussion Question 2 in Chapter 4, how might Darwinian algorithms relate to the development of kin recognition templates?

ANSWER KEY FOR MULTIPLE-CHOICE QUESTIONS

1.	c	6.	a
2.	a	7.	c
3.	e	8.	e
4.	d	9.	b
5.	b	10.	e

| Cooperation

DISCUSSION QUESTIONS

1. Read G. Wilkinson's (1984) article, "Reciprocal food sharing in vampire bats," in Nature *(vol. 308, pp. 181–184). Then outline how Wilkinson was able to separate out the effects of kinship and reciprocity in his study of vampire bats.*

In the introduction of Wilkinson's article, he primes us for the task at hand by describing the fascinating social behavior of vampire bats. A few aspects of vampire bat sociality are especially important in separating the effects of kinship and reciprocity: (1) male vampire bats abandon the social group when they mature, (2) female vampire bats usually remain within the maternal group, (3) female vampire groups are most often composed of close relatives, and (4) blood meals are shared with individuals in the group that have failed to feed. Given these characteristics, one might expect it to be particularly difficult to tease kinship and **reciprocity** apart in terms of their contribution to cooperative food sharing in vampire bats—that is, their regurgitation of blood meals for other bats. Nevertheless, Wilkinson used two clever techniques, one statistical and one experimental, to show that both relatedness and reciprocity can act within vampire social groups. First, Wilkinson estimated relatedness by subjecting known bloodlines (e.g., individual a is the daughter of individual b who is the daughter of individual c) to rigorous statistical inquiry. Wilkinson also measured the potential for reciprocity by calculating a coefficient of association for each individual; because reciprocity depends on repeated interactions between individuals within a group, this coefficient of association essentially quantifies how often two group members were seen together. Once the coefficients of relatedness and association were calculated for each individual, Wilkinson asked how well each coefficient predicted the incidence of food sharing in vampire bats. Statistically speaking, it turned out that vampire bats were significantly more likely to share blood meals with close relatives than distant relatives and to share with close associates than with unfamiliar conspecifics. These data suggest that both kinship and reciprocity can modulate cooperative interactions. Wilkinson argued that several aspects of vampire bat feeding and social behavior would favor reciprocal food sharing: (1) vampire bat natural history (e.g., blood-sharing behavior, mortality rates) suggest that there would be ample opportunity for repeated interactions, (2) the benefits of receiving food are likely to outweigh the costs of sharing, and (3) vampire bats appear to be able to distinguish roostmates from strangers. To strengthen his statistical argument for the importance of reciprocity, Wilkinson constructed a group of vampire bats consisting of nine individuals (four females from one roost, three females from a different roost, one infant, and one male). It is important to note that in the experimental group females from the same roost were not close kin, but they were close associates, and that the lone male was not closely associated with any of his experimental groupmates. This type of design all but eliminates the effects of kin on reciprocal food sharing. The key question, then, is whether individuals preferentially share blood meals with unrelated associates. Indeed, Wilkinson found that (1) individuals most often share blood with roostmates (e.g., of the thirteen regurgitations recorded, twelve occurred between individuals from the same roost), (2) individuals that received food were more likely to regurgitate blood meals for individuals that had previously donated to them, and (3) the only individual that failed to receive blood meals (even when in dire need) was the male who, as you should recall, was the only individual without some close associations within the group. All in all, Wilkinson's statistical and experimental analyses demonstrate that reciprocity can influence the cooperative tendencies of vampire bats above and beyond what one might expect from kinship alone.

2. *Run a small prisoner's dilemma experiment with a few other students. In one group, using coins as payoffs, test pairs of subjects (who cannot communicate with each other in any manner) and tell them beforehand that they will only play this game once. In a second treatment, use pairs of subjects (who cannot communicate with each other) but inform them that they will play this game many, many times together, but do not tell them exactly how many times. In a third and fourth treatment, repeat treatments 1 and 2, but allow the subjects to communicate with each other before the game starts. What sort of differences and similarities do you predict across treatments? What do the data say?*

When designing your **prisoner's dilemma** experiment, you should be aware of the participants' previous knowledge. Classmates should probably be excluded from this experiment because they are likely to be familiar with the expectations of the prisoner's dilemma game, which may influence the way they play the game (e.g., the frequency of cooperation and defection). Thus, naive students should be recruited for your experiment. The first pair of experiments mimic standard game theoretical treatments of reciprocity, so let's use the same payoff matrix that was provided in Tables 9.1 and 9.2 of the text. If the game is played only once (treatment 1), we might predict that the students will defect under all circumstances. To understand this, recall that it always pays to defect, regardless of the strategy of your opponent *when there is no opportunity for reciprocity*—that is, when the game is played just once, cheaters will exploit cooperators and benefit from doing so. But if the players are allowed to interact repeatedly and if the players are capable of remembering past moves and adjusting their behavior accordingly (as is likely in most humans), we might expect a different dynamic. Recall that the *dilemma* arises because, although each *individual* does best to cheat, the greatest *mutual* benefit (e.g., coins) comes when both individuals cooperate rather than when both individuals cheat. When a pair of subjects play the game many, many times and cannot communicate, we might predict that some form of mutual cooperation emerges via for instance, a tit-for-tat-like strategy (also see generous tit-for-tat, Pavlov, image scoring, and good standing strategies in Wedekind and Milinski, 1996, 2000; Milinski and Wedekind, 1998; Milinski et al., 2001).

In the second pair of experiments, you allow the subjects to communicate with one another before the game starts. The design of experiments 3 and 4 relies on your definition of communication. As you will see in Chapter 12, communication is generally defined as the transfer of information between signaler and receiver. For our purposes, communication can take two forms: (1) unintended communication between a signaler and receiver—for example, subject 2 gathers information about subject 1's coin stash by cueing in on the "jingling" of coins and responds accordingly during the game, and (2) intended communication between a signaler and receiver that allows for the development of pre-experimental strategies. Although it might be important to assess partner quality per se before or during the cooperative interaction (Leimar, 1997), we shall focus on the latter form of communication. Imagine that your participants are naive to the hypotheses that you are testing but that they understand the payoffs associated with cooperation and defection. When communication is added to the equation, should we expect the players in treatment 3 to unconditionally defect as they did in treatment 1? Maybe not. If communication allows the players to reach some sort of compromise before the game begins (e.g., if we both cooperate, we both can reap some sort of benefit), we might expect the frequency of mutual cooperation to increase in treatment 3 relative to treatment 1. Indeed, communication of this sort appears to foster mutually beneficial decision-making in humans, even when the game represents a one-shot deal such as trading or bargaining interactions (Sally, 1995; McGinn et al., 2003). Alternatively, we might hypothesize that pre-game communication should increase the incidence of cooperator-defector pairs. If two individuals manufacture a verbal agreement to cooperate, the temptation for one individual to cheat may be even higher than in treatment 1. Let's say that in treatment 1, the probability that subject 1 will defect or cooperate is about 50 percent. Regardless of subject 1's decision, subject 2 benefits from cheating. In treatment 3, however, the probability that subject 1 cooperates may be enhanced based on pre-game consultation with subject 2. In such circumstances, it may pay subject 2 to deceive its partner—that is, renege on the initial agreement, especially since he never has to interact with this partner again. What would we predict for circumstances where communication is allowed but individuals interact repeatedly? Here it might not benefit subject 2 to denounce the original cooperative bargain because subject 1 might retaliate on the next move by cheating, a situation that could quickly lead to neither subject obtaining benefits during the game. Given the costs to cheating in an iterated game and the potential for pre-game strategizing, it is possible that the frequency of mutual cooperation in treatment 4 might exceed that which was observed in treatment 2.

3. How would you respond to the following statement: Animals aren't capable of human-like thought processes and therefore they cannot be cooperating.

Merriam Webster's Collegiate Dictionary defines cooperation as "an association of *persons* for common benefit." Clearly, the fact that nonhuman animals *can* cooperate has not yet taken hold, despite the fact that powerful evidence exists to the contrary in taxa ranging from invertebrates to primates (as was illustrated throughout this chapter). Indeed, some may argue spiritedly that cooperation must require human-like thought processes or complex cognitive abilities (e.g., compassion, image-scoring, vast long-term memory). This argument, however, can be derailed if we consider that (1) only one path to cooperation—reciprocity—requires the ability to recognize individuals and remember specific events (e.g., individual *a* shared a blood meal but individual *b* did not; see also Dugatkin, 2002), and (2) complex thought processes are sufficient *but not necessary* for reciprocity to emerge. First, let's focus on condition (1). As discussed in the chapter, neither byproduct mutualism nor group selection hinges on the ability to recognize individuals or remember past events. Drawing on an example from the text, imagine that a large boulder traps you and a friend and that certain death looms unless both of you pool your energy to remove the boulder. Is there really any incentive to sit back and watch as your friend tries helplessly to clear the boulder? No! Thus, cooperation is simply a byproduct of the selfish tendencies of both you and your friend—both of you act to prevent your fitness from plummeting to zero, which is likely if the boulder is not removed. With respect to group selection, cooperation evolves because groups of altruists produce more offspring than groups composed primarily of selfish individuals—that is, between-group selection. Based on these abbreviated descriptions, it should be apparent that neither byproduct mutualism nor group selection calls for complex cognitive mechanisms. Now, let's turn our attention to condition (2). Claiming that animals are incapable of cooperation boils down to a failure to recognize that animals do, in fact, possess cognitive machinery *sufficient* to make cooperation work. For reciprocity to occur, animals need to recognize past interactants and remember which individuals cooperated and which individuals did not. Individual recognition can be accomplished via visual, olfactory, acoustic, electrical, or mechanosensory cues, and it has been demonstrated in both a large number of taxa and in many different contexts (e.g., mate choice, aggression, territoriality, cooperation). Remembering whether a particular individual cooperated in the past does not necessarily require long-term memory, particularly when the frequency of interaction between two individuals is high. In such situations, working (short-term) memory may be sufficient to promote the cooperative enterprise, and it is likely that short-term memory plays a critical role in the dynamics of cooperative games (Milinski and Wedekind, 1998). Taken together, conditions (1) and (2) refute the notion that cooperation can only occur when human-like thought processes exist.

4. Why do you suppose that work on animal behavior and cooperation draws more attention from other disciplines, such as mathematics, political science, and psychology, than any other area in ethology? What might we learn about human cooperation from studies of animal cooperation? What sorts of things would be difficult to glean about human cooperation by studying animal cooperation?

Cooperation infiltrates virtually every aspect of human society, from the interactions of children in a sandbox and online trading auctions to associations between powerful nations. Given the inherent appeal of cooperation (as opposed to conflict) and the fact that cooperative tentacles penetrate the lives of nonhuman and human animals alike, it is no wonder that ethological examinations of cooperation have drawn significant attention in other fields. Indeed, if you search for literature on the prisoner's dilemma game, you are certain to find fascinating articles in journals with foci as diverse as economics, political science, social science, animal behavior, mathematics, and psychology. As you have observed throughout this book, other aspects of ethology have been successfully applied to human social behavior (e.g., kinship) but arguably without as much fervor as cooperation. The question then is how studies on cooperation in nonhuman animals might be important for understanding human cooperation. One answer to this question is that by studying nonhuman animals and documenting similarities and differences in cooperative behavior among taxa, we can better understand the phylogenetic trajectories of cooperation. In doing so, we might be able to pinpoint the social or ecological conditions that favored the evolution of certain patterns of cooperation in humans. Furthermore, although it is unlikely that any one example of nonhuman animal cooperation will apply in full to human cooperation, each provides a glimpse of what sorts of factors may promote cooperation in our species (e.g., intimate groups in which interaction frequency is high; situations where the benefits of cooperating far exceed the costs of defecting). Indeed, one could argue that studying cooperation in nonhuman animals provides a wealth of baseline statistics, which may ultimately aid in generating predictions about what types of groups (e.g., small, stable with a high degree of familiarity among groupmates) might fare best under circumstances where cooperation is seemingly paramount (e.g., on the battlefield). What sorts of things would be difficult to glean about human cooperation by studying animal cooperation? First, it may not be possible to know the motivational underpinnings of cooperation or defection in nonhuman animals. After all, we cannot *ask* a guppy why it chose to cooperate on round 1 of a predator inspection bout but defect on round 2. Second, some forms of human cooperation may rely on certain sets of rules and mores that are exclusively human. Of course, this is not entirely unexpected, given that humans have been exposed to different selection pressures over time and to a social milieu that differs in many respects from any other animal. Thus, despite the powerful predictions spawned by studies of cooperation in nonhuman animals, we also need to consider how the cooperative enterprise has evolved in the context of human sociality.

MULTIPLE-CHOICE QUESTIONS

1. The required relationship among payoffs in the prisoner's dilemma game, where S = sucker's payoff, R = reward for mutual cooperation, P = punishment for mutual defection, and T = temptation to cheat, is
   a. $S > R > P > T$.
   b. $R > P > T > S$.
   c. $T > P > R > S$.
   d. $P > S > T > P$.
   e. $T > R > P > S$.

2. The four paths to the evolution and maintenance of cooperation in animals are:
   a. group selection, trait-group selection, kin selection, and reproductive skew.
   b. kin selection, group selection, reciprocity, and byproduct mutualism.
   c. byproduct mutualism, tit-for-tat, prisoner's dilemma, and heritability.
   d. group selection, ecological constraints theory, tit-for-tat, and sensory exploitation.
   e. kin selection, truncation selection, natural selection, and within-group selection.

3. Which of the following is *not* a characteristic of the tit-for-tat rule?
   a. Players utilize conditionally cooperative strategies.
   b. Players using the tit-for-tat strategy remember three moves back.
   c. Players using the tit-for-tat strategy never defect first.
   d. Players interact repeatedly.
   e. Players using the tit-for-tat strategy copy their partner's previous move.

4. Studies conducted by Naomi Pierce and her colleagues on the relationship between the imperial blue butterfly (*Jalmenus evagoras*) and the ant (*Iridomyrmex anceps*) demonstrated
   a. a mutualistic relationship between butterfly pupae/larvae and the ants.
   b. that the mutualism provided significant survival benefits to the butterflies and substantial nutritive benefits to the ants.
   c. that the butterflies incur substantial costs by producing sugary solutions for the ants.
   d. that ants and butterfly pupae/larvae communicate via vibrational cues.
   e. all of the above

5. Byproduct mutualism (BM) differs from reciprocity (REC) in which of the following ways?
   a. Scorekeeping is not required in BM or REC, but there is a temptation to cheat in REC.
   b. In REC, but not BM, there is no temptation to cheat nor do individuals have to keep track of their partner's behavior.
   c. There is no temptation to cheat in BM or REC, but scorekeeping is required in REC.
   d. In BM, but not REC, there is no temptation to cheat nor do individuals have to keep track of their partner's behavior.
   e. There is no temptation to cheat in BM or REC, but scorekeeping is required in BM.

6. Which of the following statements about group selection is *false*?
   a. Some variation in the proportion of cooperators and selfish phenotypes must exist among groups.
   b. Between-group selection favors cooperation in kin groups but favors selfish phenotypes in nonkin groups.
   c. A key aspect of group selection models is that natural selection operates both within and between groups.
   d. Between-group selection favors cooperation if groups with more cooperators outreproduce groups with fewer cooperators.
   e. Within-group selection always favors selfish phenotypes because they receive benefits without paying the costs of altruism.

7. What is the "dilemma" in the prisoner's dilemma game?
   a. It pays each individual to cheat every time, but mutual defection is more costly than mutual cooperation.
   b. Individuals cannot choose the proper strategy because the payoffs constantly change.
   c. All strategies provide equal payoffs regardless of what one's partner does.
   d. Cooperation can never evolve despite the fact that individuals always do best when cooperating.

e. The payoff for cooperating is substantially higher than the payoff for cheating unless both individuals in a pair opt to cheat.

8. Which of the following statements applies to the cooperative breeding system of dwarf mongooses (*Helogale parvula*)?
   a. The dominant male and female in the group sire only 10 percent of the total offspring in a group.
   b. The number of matings obtained is inversely correlated with rank in both sexes.
   c. Dwarf mongooses are considered to be plural breeders.
   d. Abundant prey and high predation rates likely contributed to the evolution of solitary lifestyles in dwarf mongooses.
   e. Subordinate animals are reproductively suppressed and cooperate in ways that increase the reproductive success of dominant individuals.

9. When coalitions exist for long periods of time, they are referred to as
   a. colonies.
   b. herds.
   c. mutualisms.
   d. alliances.
   e. societies.

10. Phylogenetic analyses allow us to examine whether cooperative behavior in many related species
   a. is under the control of genes that follow Mendel's law of segregation.
   b. is a fixed trait that can no longer be subject to natural selection.
   c. can be explained by common ancestry rather than independent selection regimes.
   d. will evolve in the future due to each species inhabiting similar environments.
   e. can be subject to rigorous mathematical treatments.

REVIEW AND CHALLENGE QUESTIONS

1. Compare and contrast the four paths to cooperation—kinship, reciprocity, byproduct mutualism, and group selection—in terms of the incentive to cheat and how this incentive influences the dynamics of the cooperative interactions.

2. Obtain a copy of Nowak and Sigmund's (1993) paper entitled "A strategy of win stay, lose shift that outperforms tit-for-tat in the prisoner's-dilemma game" in *Nature* (vol. 364, pp. 56–58). Describe how their strategy—dubbed Pavlov—differs from the tit-for-tat strategy that was introduced in this chapter. What are the defining features of the Pavlov strategy that allow it to outcompete tit-for-tat?

3. In the discussion of cooperation via group selection, you learned that group-level benefits could be realized only under circumstances where there is variation in the frequency of cooperators among groups. Why must this be so? Could evolutionary forces act at the group level without such variation?

4. Why are phylogenetic analyses important for understanding the evolution of cooperative behavior—or any other behavior—in animals? What insights might we gain from conducting phylogenetic analyses in concert with empirical research in behavioral ecology?

5. In this chapter, you encountered some stimulating examples of coalition and alliance formation in baboons and dolphins. Oftentimes, coalition formation involves one animal intervening in aggressive disputes between others. Under what circumstances would it be beneficial for a dominant animal to intervene in fights between other group members? Can you think of any circumstances in which it benefits subordinate animals to intervene?

ANSWER KEY FOR MULTIPLE-CHOICE QUESTIONS

1.	e	6.	b
2.	b	7.	a
3.	b	8.	e
4.	e	9.	d
5.	d	10.	c

CHAPTER 10 | Foraging

DISCUSSION QUESTIONS

1. Read R. Pulliam's 1973 article, "On the advantages of flocking," in the Journal of Theoretical Biology *(vol. 38, pp. 419–422). Based on the article, outline the "many eyes" hypothesis and discuss how it relates to foraging behavior.*

Prior to Pulliam's article, some authors proposed that "peripheral predation" would favor flocking behavior. To understand this, consider the possible angles of approach that could lead to successful capture of a prey item by a predator. Does the predator have a greater chance of seizing a given forager when that individual feeds alone or when that individual is surrounded by other foragers? Clearly, the probability of effectively capturing a given prey item decreases as group size increases because each individual is essentially shielded by its group-mates. Early theoretical work on flocking suggested that any forager that moves toward its neighbors would reduce the possibility of being captured. But Pulliam recognized that if individuals on the periphery of the flock were more likely to be captured than individuals at the center of the flock, then it might be best for peripheral animals to leave the flock and forage alone. This, in turn, could lead to the dissolution of the flock. Pulliam's model highlighted another important factor that could favor flocking—increased probability of predator detection—and sought to determine whether flocks provide individuals with a level of predator detection that they could not achieve when alone. Lima (1995) articulated Pulliam's logic quite well in saying: "As group size increases in socially foraging animals, there are progressively more eyes scanning the environment for predators. Therefore, as group size increases, an individual forager can devote less time to vigilance without any lessening of the group's collective ability to detect an attack." Using a simple model, Pulliam found that for a given probability of detecting one predator approach incident (e.g., 0.87), solitary animals would need to scan at a higher rate (e.g., 12 scans per minute) than animals occupying a flock (e.g., in a flock of four individuals; 3 scans per minute). Furthermore, when many successive predator approaches are considered, solitary individuals have astonishingly low probabilities of detecting each predator relative to animals in flocks (e.g., for five predator approaches, the probability of detecting all five turns out to be 0.01 for individuals and 0.48 for animals in four-member flocks). It should now be relatively clear that foraging in flocks is advantageous from the perspective of predator detection. How does this relate to foraging success? The key to answering this question is to recognize that animals have a set time budget that they must partition among daily activities such as feeding, mating, vigilance, and so on. Flocking reduces the time that any one individual must spend looking out for predators, thus allowing each animal within the flock to devote more time to foraging without experiencing an increased risk of being captured. Despite the heuristic value of Pulliam's model and the **many eyes hypothesis**, there still remains some debate about their applicability to flocking behavior under natural settings (e.g., Lima, 1995; Roberts, 1996). For a very recent treatment of this topic and related issues, consult a review by Beauchamp (2003) and its associated discussion and commentary articles.

2. *Read E. L. Charnov's 1976 article, "Optimal foraging, the marginal value theorem," in* Theoretical Population Biology *(vol. 9, pp. 129–136). How might you modify the model to examine other behaviors displayed by animals?*

Charnov's paper used an optimization approach to examine how foragers make use of patchily distributed resources given changes in the quality of a patch over time (e.g., food intake rate), the average food intake rate for the habitat, and the distance between patches. In the "Basic OFT: What to Eat and Where to Eat It" section of this chapter and in Discussion Question 5, you were introduced to some of the most salient predictions of Charnov's marginal value theorem, including: (1) foragers should remain in a patch until the marginal rate of intake is equal to the average intake rate across all patches in the environment, (2) in habitats composed of patches of similar quality, animals should spend more time in each patch as the distance between patches increases, and (3) when patches are uniformly distributed, animals should spend more time in each patch as patch quality increases. To understand how the **marginal value theorem** can be applied to behavior outside the realm of foraging, we must recognize a few general, but essential, properties of Charnov's model. First, the resource in question should be patchily distributed—that is, discontinuous. Second, animals are expected to spend a certain amount of time and energy depleting the resources available in a given patch, which constitutes an investment cost. Third, animals amass additional time costs when traveling from patch to patch in search of resources. Fourth, animals should accumulate some form of fitness benefit while in a patch; for foragers, this fitness benefit comes in the form of food and energy.

What sorts of other behaviors might be amenable to investigation using the marginal value theorem as a template? Parker and Stuart (1976) provided a compelling example in their exploration of optimal copulation duration in male dungflies (*Scatophaga stercoraria*). Parker and colleagues have studied dungflies for the greater part of thirty years and have unveiled many interesting aspects of dungfly natural history. Male dungflies congregate on fresh manure where they wait for the arrival of females. Females visit these droppings only to mate and deposit eggs. Aside from virgins, many of the arriving females will contain sperm, which has been stored from their copulations at different patches of manure. Luckily for the male suitors, the sperm of past males can be displaced during copulation with the female *and* the probability of successfully fertilizing eggs increases with copulation duration. Parker and his colleagues have demonstrated that the relationship between copulation duration and fertilization gains approximates the cumulative gain function described in Charnov (1973)—that is, the males experience diminishing returns such that the number of *additional* eggs fertilized decreases with copulation duration. Do the general properties of Charnov's model apply to the dungfly system? Yes! First, eggs are distributed patchily—each female represents a patch in this case. Second, males spend time and energy gaining access to available eggs (e.g., time spent copulating, energy from sperm investment, energy from fending off other males that attempt to disrupt copulation). Third, males experience substantial search costs (e.g., intervening time between copulations, energy expended traveling between patches), particularly when many males compete for access to newly arrived females. Fourth, males accumulate fitness benefits during copulation in the form of progeny. Using Figure 10.9 (see text, p. 350) as a template, let's plot the cumulative gain function and establish the optimum copulation duration for a given search time. The x-axis is split in half, with search time on the left side and copulation duration on the right side. The y-axis represents fertilization gains—that is, the proportion of eggs fertilized by a new suitor. By drawing a tangent line from our estimated search time to the cumulative gain function, we can determine the optimal copulation duration (OCD):

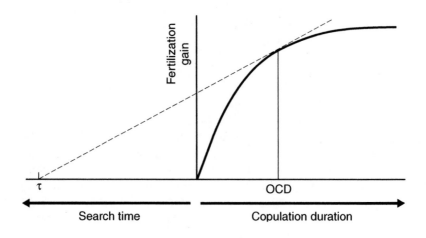

We have applied Charnov's marginal value theorem to copulation duration in dungflies. Our example is a simplified version of Parker and Stuart's (1976) original theoretical work, which was formulated independent of Charnov's model. If this example strikes your fancy, some recent modifications to the model and some additional empirical work spawned from Parker's laboratory may also be of interest (Parker et al., 1993; Parker and Simmons, 1994; Charnov and Parker, 1995; Parker et al., 1999). Of course, dungfly copulation is only one of many possible applications of the marginal value theorem. You are encouraged to peruse the literature for additional marvels of animal behavior that fit nicely within the framework of optimal foraging theory.

3. Using Math Box 10.1 as a starting point, construct a foraging model with three prey types. Imagine that you already know that it pays for a forager to eat prey type 1 and prey type 2. What are the conditions under which it should add prey type 3?

To determine the conditions under which our hypothetical forager should add a third prey item, we will use the same notation as Math Box 10.1 (see pp. 346–347 of the text):

e_i = energy provided by prey type i
h_i = handling associated with prey type i
λ_i = encounter rate with prey type i
T_s = amount of time devoted to searching for prey
T = total time
E = total energy

Equation (4) from Math Box 10.1 represents the net energy per unit time (E/T) associated with taking two prey items:

$$\frac{E}{T} \; (2) = \frac{\lambda_1 e_1 + \lambda_2 e_2}{1 + \lambda_1 h_1 + \lambda_2 h_2}$$

Based on equations (1) and (3) in Math Box 10.1, we can formulate an equality that represents the net energy per unit time (E/T) associated with taking three prey items:

$$\frac{E}{T} \; (3) = \frac{T_s(\lambda_1 e_1 + \lambda_2 e_2 + \lambda_3 e_3)}{T_s + T_s \lambda_1 h_1 + T_s \lambda_2 h_2 + T_s \lambda_3 h_3}$$

Using the conventions shown in Math Box 10.1 (factoring out the T_s), the above equation can be reduced to:

$$\frac{E}{T} \; (3) = \frac{\lambda_1 e_1 + \lambda_2 e_2 + \lambda_3 e_3}{1 + \lambda_1 h_1 + \lambda_2 h_2 + \lambda_3 h_3}$$

What conditions would favor a predator that takes only two prey items? Generally speaking, taking two prey items instead of three will be favored when the net energy gain per unit time associated with two prey items exceeds the net energy gain per unit time associated with three prey items:

$\frac{E}{T}(2) > \frac{E}{T}(3)$, which can be expanded based on the above equations to read:

$$\frac{\lambda_1 e_1 + \lambda_2 e_2}{1 + \lambda_1 h_1 + \lambda_2 h_2} > \frac{\lambda_1 e_1 + \lambda_2 e_2 + \lambda_3 e_3}{1 + \lambda_1 h_1 + \lambda_2 h_2 + \lambda_3 h_3}$$

After a fair bit of careful algebra, we can show that this inequality reduces to:

$$\frac{\lambda_1 e_1 + \lambda_2 e_2}{1 + \lambda_1 h_1 + \lambda_2 h_2} > \frac{e_3}{h_3}$$

The steps involved in achieving the above inequality were as follows:
a. Cross-multiply to eliminate the fractions.
b. Using subtractive methods, remove terms that are common to both sides of the equation.
c. λ_3 is common to all terms and can be eliminated by dividing both sides of the equation by λ_3.
d. Move all terms with h_3 to one side of the equation and all terms with e_3 to the other side.
e. Divide through by h_3 and by $(1 + \lambda_1 h_1 + \lambda_2 h_2)$ to yield the final inequality.

Notice that the fraction on the left side of the inequality is the net energy gain per unit time for taking two prey items, yielding a simplified inequality:

$$\frac{E}{T}(2) > \frac{e_3}{h_3}$$

Thus, whenever the net energy gain per unit time associated with taking two prey items exceeds the profitability of a third prey item (e_3/h_3), the predator should stick with two prey items. However, if the profitability of the third prey item is sufficiently high to render the above inequality untrue (e.g., third prey item that is easy to capture, immobilize, and ingest, and that has high caloric content), then the predator should opt to add prey item 3 to its diet. Similar to what you encountered in Math Box 10.1, the decision to add the third prey item does *not* depend on how common prey type 3 is—that is, on prey type 3's encounter rate (λ_3).

It is important to note that our solution is qualitatively different from that provided in Math Box 10.1. In the Math Box, inequality (5) was solved to show that the encounter rate of prey item 1 (λ_1) is critical for determining whether an animal should add additional prey items to its diet—that is, when a threshold encounter rate with prey 1 is achieved, it alone should be taken. When the same algebraic manipulations used in Math Box 10.1 are attempted for the case of three prey items, the solution is a bit more difficult to interpret. Nevertheless, you are encouraged to give it a whirl. Here are some tips for implementing similar algebraic procedures as Math Box 10.1:

a. Cross-multiply to eliminate the fractions.
b. Using subtractive methods, remove terms that are common to both sides of the equation.
c. λ_3 is common to all terms and can be eliminated by dividing both sides of the equation by λ_3.
d. Move all terms with λ_1 or λ_2 to one side of the equation, and keep e_3 on the other side.
e. Group terms with λ_1 and terms with λ_2, simplify, and solve.

4. Why do you suppose it took so long for ethologists and psychologists to recognize the larger literature on foraging behavior that exists in the other field? What do you think were the biggest differences in the way foraging was studied across these disciplines?

The discussion questions in Chapter 4 (Learning) introduced you to the advantages of fusing psychological paradigms with evolutionary tenets and emphasized how cross-talk between psychology and evolutionary ethology can foster our understanding of what and how animals learn. Although there has been a recent surge of empirical work that integrates psychological and evolutionary principles, the two fields differ in the types of questions they ask. With respect to foraging, a psychologist might ask questions that focus on learning mechanisms:

What learning rules do animals use to estimate patch quality?
Do memory windows or forgetting functions limit the ability of an animal to integrate past information about patch quality or location with more recent information?
Do animals have limited capacity to distinguish patches of different quality?

When faced with a similar set of foraging behaviors, ethologists might ask questions that focus on evolutionary consequences:

How long should an animal stay in a patch to maximize net energy gain?
What are the fitness costs and benefits associated with certain foraging strategies?
How does an animal partition its time between foraging and other fitness-related activities?

Both sets of questions are interesting in their own right. But if we were to construct a Venn diagram of the foraging literature over the past fifty years, we would likely see only a small region of overlap between the two sets of questions. The reason for such little overlap may be that psychologists and evolutionary ethologists have different objectives when it comes to studying foraging behavior, and they therefore utilize distinct experimental paradigms. Fortunately, times are changing and a merger between psychological and evolutionary principles has begun (see references in the "Learning and Foraging" section of the chapter).

5. *Using the graphs in Figure 10.9 as a starting point, examine what happens to the time an animal should spend in the patch as a function of how profitable that patch is. This will involve changing the shape of the curve that describes food intake as a function of patch residence time and examining what this change does to optimal time in a patch.*

To begin this exercise, let's draw a graph similar to Figure 10.9 (on p. 350 of the text). Instead of drawing just one cumulative gain function that represents average patch quality, however, we will draw two cumulative gain functions, each corresponding to a separate patch of food. Patch A will represent a high-quality patch, while Patch B will represent a low-quality patch. The x-axis is split in half with travel time (τ) on the left side and time spent in a patch on the right side. To address how the optimal time spent in a patch changes with patch quality, let's keep travel time (τ) constant—that is, the tangent lines that you draw will originate from the same point on the travel time axis. The graph you draw might look something like this:

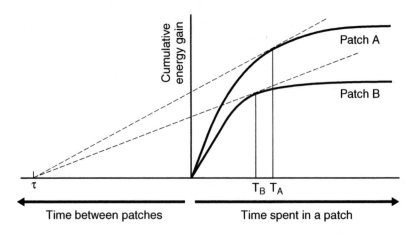

When the time it takes to travel between patches remains constant, patch quality determines the threshold time spent in a given patch. Specifically, as patch quality increases, the optimal time spent in the patch also increases. Notice that our hypothetical animal spends more time in high-quality patch A (T_A) than in low-quality patch B (T_B). This is precisely what we would expect from our knowledge of foraging behavior. Assuming that the forager depletes the food in each patch at a similar rate, patch B will approach the environmental average for marginal rate of food intake more rapidly than patch A. Thus, individuals should emigrate from patch B sooner.

MULTIPLE-CHOICE QUESTIONS

1. Optimization techniques are used to
   a. represent perfectly the conditions an animal experiences in nature.
   b. predict the best possible solution to a problem within a given set of constraints.
   c. identify which descendants of a certain individual are optimally suited to reproduce.
   d. evaluate the logic underlying the assumptions of mathematical models.
   e. determine the best possible experimental design for any given question in animal behavior.

2. Individuals that adopt "producer" foraging strategies
   a. make their own food and create innovative ways to combine food items.
   b. parasitize the foraging efforts of other group members.
   c. locate and gain access to food items in a patch.
   d. teach juveniles efficient foraging techniques.
   e. produce chemicals that inhibit competitors from feeding in the same area.

3. Public information can be beneficial in group-living animals because it allows
   a. individuals to use the behavior of others as a cue to changes in environmental conditions.
   b. animals to use the foraging success of others as an estimate of patch quality.
   c. individuals to acquire specific novel behaviors that enhance foraging success.
   d. group members to reduce environmental uncertainty.
   e. a, b, and d

4. Which of the following statements regarding Toma and colleagues' work on the *per* gene and foraging in honeybees is *false*?
   a. *per* gene mRNA expression was greatest in young bees that remained at the nest.
   b. the *per* gene was used as a candidate gene involved in the control of developmental changes to foraging behavior.
   c. *per* gene mRNA expression was quantified in their study.
   d. young, precocious foragers had similar *per* mRNA levels as typical, older foragers.
   e. studies were conducted in both laboratory and natural populations of honeybees.

5. The simplest optimal prey choice models assume that
   a. foragers cannot simultaneously handle one prey item and search for another.
   b. all prey items are encountered by a forager simultaneously.
   c. foragers maximize their rate of energy intake.
   d. *x* units of time are required to accurately identify prey items.
   e. a and c

6. Models that examine whether the variance in food intake rates affects foraging decisions are called
   a. marginal value models.
   b. optimal prey choice models.
   c. risk-sensitive optimal foraging models.
   d. specific nutrient constraint models.
   e. public information models.

7. Which of the following statements does *not* apply to Belovsky's study of specific nutrient constraints in moose?
   a. Sodium is scare and required in large amounts by vertebrates.
   b. Terrestrial plants provide more energy, but less sodium than aquatic plants.
   c. Moose can store sodium, which allows them to survive over the winter when aquatic plants are unavailable.
   d. A moose should spend approximately 81 percent of its summer foraging time on aquatic plants.
   e. A linear programming model was developed to predict moose foraging behavior.

8. The "marginal value" refers to the
   a. average rate of food intake across all available patches.
   b. average distance between patches.
   c. rate of intake associated with the next prey item in the current patch.
   d. absolute number of food items, regardless of quality, in a given patch.
   e. degree to which food items are clumped versus uniformly distributed in a patch.

9. The most salient prediction of optimal prey choice models is that the decision to add a less profitable prey item (prey type 2) to one's diet depends on
   a. handling associated with prey type 1.
   b. handling associated with prey type 2.
   c. encounter rate of prey type 2.
   d. search time devoted to two versus one prey item.
   e. encounter rate of prey type 1.

10. A "patch" is defined as a clump of resources that
    a. fulfills only an animal's sodium requirement.

b. is constantly and immediately renewed.
c. is inaccessible to foragers.
d. cannot be depleted by foragers.
e. none of the above.

REVIEW AND CHALLENGE QUESTIONS

1. Discuss the primary differences between social learning and public information models of foraging. In addition, consider the large body of work that has focused on what has been dubbed the information center hypothesis (see "Communication Venues—Foraging" in Chapter 12). Which of the two models—public information or social learning—is most applicable to the information center hypothesis?

2. As described in the chapter, Healey and Krebs (1992) examined the relationship between hippocampal volume and food-storing behavior in seven species of corvid birds. The authors found a strong positive correlation between hippocampal volume and the extent to which these birds store food—that is, the hippocampus was larger in species that stored large quantities of food. Do these data provide conclusive evidence that the hippocampus is responsible for aspects of foraging related to spatial memory? If so, support your answer. If not, design an experiment that could shed light on the relationship between the hippocampus and food-storing behavior.

3. Describe how risk-sensitive foraging strategies might be manifest in a population of foragers. Can you think of any variables, aside from hunger, that might influence whether an individual chooses to forage using risk-prone or risk-averse strategies?

4. Based on what you have learned in this chapter, do you think molecular, neurobiological, and physiological techniques will significantly advance our understanding of foraging behavior in years to come? Discuss several aspects of foraging behavior that might be amenable to research that employs such techniques.

5. Imagine that you are studying two populations of tropical lizards that inhabit areas where high-quality food items are distributed patchily—that is, it would take some time to travel from patch to patch. Lizard population A inhabits an area with high predation risk (e.g., many birds of prey), while lizard population B inhabits an area with low predation risk (e.g., few birds of prey). How might you expect foraging patterns to differ between these two lizard populations with respect to the time spent in a given patch? Construct your argument by modifying what you have learned about the marginal value theorem.

ANSWER KEY FOR MULTIPLE-CHOICE QUESTIONS

1.	b	6.	c
2.	c	7.	d
3.	e	8.	c
4.	a	9.	e
5.	e	10.	e

| Antipredator Behavior

DISCUSSION QUESTIONS

1. Pick your animal of choice, and sketch what a normal time budget (how much time it spends feeding, sleeping, mating, and so on) might look like for this animal. Now, besides the direct time spent looking for predators, examine how predation might directly or indirectly affect all the behaviors on your time budget.

The behavioral mosaic of any given animal might include patrolling territorial boundaries, engaging in overt aggressive interactions with territorial intruders, searching for and handling food items, courting potential mates, grooming, and sleeping. Let's investigate how predation risk could influence each of these behaviors in turn.

a. *Territory patrols.* Territory holders patrol their boundaries to prevent upstart conspecifics from intruding upon (or commandeering) sections of the territory. Sometimes, patrolling animals will move along large sections of open land, thereby making themselves conspicuous to aerial and terrestrial predators. Predation risk may impose limitations on the efficiency of these patrolling bouts. For instance, territory holders may opt to patrol only those portions of the territory that provide cover, reduce total patrolling time, or patrol faster. In any case, territorial animals may fail to evict intruders when predation risk is relatively high. Predation pressure may also affect the size and location of the territory (Eason and Stamps, 1992).

b. *Overt aggressive interactions.* Animal contests involve a series of conspicuous displays (e.g., increasing apparent size) and, under certain circumstances, highly escalated fighting tactics (see Chapter 14). Animals cannot dedicate time to vigilance while fighting. In addition, escalated fighting tactics may make the contestants more visible to predators. Animals may opt to forego aggressive contests, settle fights by less escalated (and less conspicuous) means, or escalate faster when predators are present. Thus, predation pressure can have pronounced effects on the dynamics of aggressive contests (Brick and Jakobsson, 2002).

c. *Foraging behavior.* As discussed in the chapter (see "Predation and Foraging" section), predation pressures can affect nearly every aspect of foraging behavior—from feeding localities and food preferences to the timing of foraging bouts.

d. *Courtship.* Predation risk may affect courtship rituals in similar ways to how it affects aggressive contests. Mating behavior often involves striking displays of color and movement, both of which might attract predators. Furthermore, courting pairs cannot allocate much time to vigilance. As such, we might expect cessation of courtship, the use of less conspicuous displays, or the use of alternative (less conspicuous) mating tactics when predators are present (Evans et al., 2002).

e. *Grooming.* To effectively groom oneself or a partner, an animal must search for and remove parasites or debris from the skin, hair, feathers, scales, and so on. In doing so, the groomer cannot spend much time being vigilant. Therefore, grooming behavior may come to a screeching halt when predation risk is high. Moreover, the locations in which or the times at which grooming is conducted may be affected by predation pressure (e.g., groom in safe locales or at safe times; Cowlishaw, 1997).

f. *Sleeping.* For an excellent example of how predation risk can affect sleeping behavior, refer to the "Sleep and Predation in Mallard Ducks" section of Chapter 3.

2. Jerison interprets an historical increase in the brain size of predators and their prey as evidence of a predator-prey arms race, where the weapon is brain power. Can you think of other alternative hypotheses that might explain this finding?

Jerison adopts an evolutionary view for the parallel increase in brain size in predators and prey (more specifically, carnivores and ungulates). In Jerison's (1970) analysis, he found that carnivores exhibited larger relative brain size than their putative ungulate prey and that this relationship has been preserved over evolutionary time (at least as far back as 40–60 million years ago). He interpreted these results as evidence for a cognitive arms race between predators and prey. Brain size in predators presumably reflects hunting prowess, while brain sizes in prey relates to their ability to escape predators. Thus, as brain size in predators increases, prey should be selected for increased brain size in order to keep pace with the ever-more efficient predators. This, in turn, initiates a selection cascade, whereby brain sizes in both predator and prey increase with evolutionary time. But this interpretation was met with some opposition (Radinsky,

1978). One alternative hypothesis that Radinsky alluded to relates to longevity (also see Austad and Fischer, 1992; Rose and Mueller, 1998, for alternative views). If increased life span is selectively advantageous across taxa (e.g., providing increased time to reproduce) and, if enhanced longevity hinges on the ability to learn from past experiences or otherwise conduct some cognitive tasks, then selection on, for instance, learning capabilities may drive selection for larger brains (e.g., leading to increased neuronal populations in certain brain regions). In this example, natural selection favors increased longevity independently across predator and prey taxa and, as a result, brain sizes appear to increase in concert. In other words, such selection might give the false impression that predators and prey are co-evolving—that is, that changes in predator brain size are inciting changes in prey brain size). In reality, however, increased longevity might be selected for in both predators and prey (e.g., via selection for increased foraging efficiency and greater learning capabilities).

A related argument might go as follows: Imagine that habitat complexity increases with time and that increased brain size allows an animal to succeed in progressively more complex environments. Under such circumstances, we might expect natural selection to favor increased brain size in both predators and prey based on their respective habitats but independent of one another. Here again, brain size in predators and prey does not co-evolve as would be predicted in the arms race postulated by Jerison.

3. Some prey, particularly birds, actually mob their predators and harass them until the predators leave. List some of the costs and benefits associated with such mobbing, and construct a hypothesis for what sorts of environments might favor mobbing.

Mobbing behavior is an effective antipredator tactic in many bird species (Naguib et al., 1999; Arnold, 2000; Descrochers et al., 2002, for some recent examples). It usually entails moving toward the predator and emitting mobbing calls or exhibiting behaviors (e.g., close-range aerial tactics) that could deter the approaching threat. The costs of mobbing include:

Time or opportunity. Time spent mobbing could be used for other fitness-related activities.

Offspring neglect. Leaving the nest could render offspring susceptible to predation.

Fatalities. Mobbing predators is a risky business as mobbers could be captured.

Energy. Mobbing vocalizations and aerial tactics may be energetically expensive to perform.

Injury. Close-range interactions with a predator may be damaging.

Although substantial costs are associated with mobbing, there are also benefits to exhibiting such behavior:

Reduce predation threat. Successful mobbing decreases mortality risk by deterring the predator.

Information gathering. If mobbing facilitates information acquisition, mobbers may be better informed about predation risk.

Indirect benefits. If young animals learn about predators by observing mobbing efforts, they may be better able to detect predation threats in the future.

Reciprocity. The initiator of a mobbing effort may gain future benefits (Krams and Krama, 2002).

Mobbing behavior should be favored when the fitness benefits associated with close-range interactions with approaching predators outweigh the costs. That being said, what environmental conditions would favor mobbing? First, let us examine the social environment. The success of any given mobbing effort could depend on the number of animals harassing the predator and this, in turn, could depend on the size of the social group. Thus, we might expect mobbing to be favored in social but not solitary species and, among social species, mobbing might be a more effective tactic when social groups are relatively large. As far as the physical environment is concerned, mobbing might be favored in open habitats where the predator can be detected, and dealt with at a distance from the nesting area. Open habitats may also facilitate group-mobbing behavior because mobbers could be easily detected by nearby conspecifics (who could join the effort). Mobbing vocalizations may also be more readily localized in open areas.

4. Abrahams and Pratt (2000) used a thyroid hormone to manipulate growth rates in the fathead minnow (Pimephales promelas). Thyroid treatment stunted growth rates, and the researchers found that such stunted individuals were less likely to risk exposure to predators to gain access to food. Why might that be? Is it possible to construct an argument that would predict the exact opposite of what was found? Also, what does this study tell you about the relationship between proximate and ultimate factors shaping antipredator behavior?

Abrahams and Pratt examined a three-tiered relationship between predation risk, foraging behavior, and growth rate in fathead minnows. First, the authors manipulated growth rate using thyroid hormone (T_3). Minnows exposed to T_3 generally experienced decreased rates of mass gain relative to control fish, and the authors found that decreased growth rates were associated with lower metabolic rates (e.g., lower rates of energy assimilation). The results of the growth rate experiment provided the opportunity to examine whether willingness to forage in areas with high predation risk is influenced by growth rate. As stated in the question, the authors found that stunted individuals with reduced appetites were less likely to risk exposure to predators to gain access to food. These results were interpreted in terms of the relationship between mortality risk and growth rate and, more generally, of the relationship between the fitness benefits and costs of foraging in the presence of a predator. For individuals with high growth rates, the benefits of foraging (e.g., rapid energy assimilation and further growth) may exceed the mortality risks. Thus, these animals gamble for food access in the presence of predators. Conversely, individuals with low growth rates may experience minimal benefits (e.g., slow energy assimilation and less growth) relative to the mortality costs, and thus choose to avoid foraging in areas where predators are present.

Based on a cost-benefit approach, it is possible to entertain a hypothesis that would predict the exact opposite of what was found by Abrahams and Pratt. Imagine that growth rate depends on efficient metabolic machinery (e.g., the conversion of foodstuff into energy) and that individuals with low growth rates must feed more to obtain their energy quota or to reach a size where they are less susceptible to predators. Alternatively, individuals with high growth rates and efficient metabolic machinery may need to feed less to achieve the same energy quota or a size that is unmanageable by predators. In this case, the fitness benefits of foraging may exceed the mortality risks for individuals with low growth rates. Given that individuals with low growth rates place a premium on foraging, they might be expected to take more risks to obtain food than individuals with high growth rates.

The study conducted by Abrahams and Pratt demonstrates the importance of examining antipredator behavior from both proximate and ultimate perspectives. *Why* do animals forage in the presence of a predator? The answer to this ultimate question can be cast in terms of the relative fitness costs and benefits of foraging—if the survival benefits of foraging in the presence of predators exceed the fitness costs, then risks should be taken to obtain food. *What* mechanisms mediate this decision? Presumably growth rate and metabolism play important roles in modulating foraging decisions in fathead minnows, and these parameters are integrally linked to physiological parameters such as thyroid hormone titers. Without understanding the proximate mechanisms underlying foraging decisions, it would be difficult to formulate hypotheses regarding why individuals with high or low growth rates take more risks in the presence of predators. In turn, without understanding why certain foraging patterns might emerge, it may be difficult to pinpoint the proximate mechanisms associated with such behavior (e.g., growth rate and metabolism).

5. *A number of studies have found that laboratory-raised animals can learn what constitutes danger by watching other animals respond to potential predators. How might such cultural transmission be employed by those interested in wildlife reintroduction programs?*

Wildlife reintroduction programs often entail gathering a small subset of threatened animals from the wild and establishing breeding programs in zoos or refuges. Within the secure boundaries of zoos and refuges, captive bred animals are not exposed to predators and thus cannot learn what constitutes an imminent predation threat. But the parents of captive-bred individuals likely had opportunities to learn about predators in the wild. Let's assume that adults with previous exposure to predators behave in stereotypical ways to danger and that captive bred youngsters can glean information about the perils of being low on the food chain by watching adults. Under such circumstances, young animals that observe how adults respond to certain predators may be better equipped to deal with predatory encounters in the wild than young animals that did not have the opportunity to observe adults (see the "Oblique Cultural Transmission" section of Chapter 5 in the text). Informed youngsters may then be more successfully reintroduced to the wild than their uninformed counterparts. As far as this example is concerned, wildlife reintroduction programs certainly benefit by recognizing the power of information transfer and the potential fitness benefits that captive reared animals might accrue by watching the behavior of experienced adults.

MULTIPLE-CHOICE QUESTIONS

1. When large groups of schooling fish move in erratic patterns within the group, and the school remains a cohesive unit, what type of antipredator tactic is being used?
   a. fountain effect
   b. predator inspection
   c. flash expansion
   d. confusion effect
   e. Trafalgar effect

2. Which of the following hypotheses has *not* been proposed to explain tail flagging behavior?
   a. It increases group cohesion.
   b. It functions primarily to appease dominant individuals and secondarily as an antipredator tactic.
   c. It informs the predator about the size of the prey group.
   d. It announces to a predator that it has been sighted and should abandon its attack.
   e. It warns conspecifics of potential dangers.

3. Mobbing refers to an antipredator tactic in which prey
   a. behave in an erratic manner so as to confuse the predator.
   b. adopt cryptic coloration patterns in order to avoid attack.
   c. retreat from the predator in large groups.
   d. produce alarm calls to warn group members.
   e. attack the predator either alone or in groups.

4. Which of the following statements does *not* relate to antipredator behavior and defense against snakes in California ground squirrels?
   a. Young squirrel pups have low serum-to-venom binding levels.
   b. Serum-to-venom binding levels increase after the pups emerge from the burrow, which corresponds with an increase in snake predation risk.
   c. High serum-to-venom binding levels indicate strong defenses against snakebites.
   d. Squirrel pups emerge from their natal burrows when they are about forty days old.
   e. Serum-to-venom binding levels in squirrel pups change only when the pups are exposed to snakes early in life.

5. When terrestrial predation pressures from snakes and wasps are strong, the tadpoles of red-eyed tree frogs should be selected to
   a. hatch early in the season.
   b. hatch only when disturbed by a predator.
   c. initiate poison production in order to deter predators.
   d. hatch later in the season.
   e. hatch early if snake predation pressures are stronger than wasp predation pressures.

6. Jerison's hypothesis concerning mammalian predator-prey interactions incorporated which of the following concepts?
   a. tradeoffs and antipredator tactics
   b. changes in brain size and arms races
   c. predator inspection and tradeoffs
   d. arms races and learning abilities
   e. social learning and forebrain neurochemistry

7. A tradeoff refers to the notion that
   a. predator and prey population sizes oscillate over time.
   b. prey that approach predators experience low survival probabilities.
   c. time or energy dedicated to one activity cannot be used for other activities.
   d. individual inspectors trade information about predators for foraging assistance.
   e. animals cannot divide their time or energy among multiple activities.

8. Which of the following represents a direct fitness consequence of learning about predators?
   a. There is increased neurogenesis in the forebrain.
   b. There are decreased stress hormone levels.
   c. There is enhanced knowledge of the environmental landscape.
   d. There are decreased mortality rates.
   e. There is increased vigilance behavior.

9. If differences in antipredator behavior between two populations of the same species inhabiting different environments were discovered, we could conclude that
   a. different selection pressures drive differences in antipredator behavior.
   b. neither natural selection nor learning explains interpopulational differences in antipredator behavior.
   c. different selection pressures and/or differences in past experience could explain interpopulational differences in antipredator behavior.
   d. a single predator species must exert different influences on the prey in each environment.
   e. differences in environmental conditions affected the experiences of the individuals, and thus the antipredator tactics that were adopted.

10. When should natural selection most strongly favor genetically coded predator identification mechanisms?
    a. in dynamic environments where predator types constantly change
    b. when the number of predatory threats are few and constant through time
    c. in stable environments with a vast number of predator types
    d. when predators can be identified easily by color patterns
    e. when few predators exist at any one time but the types of predator constantly change

Review and Challenge Questions

1. Vigilance entails keeping an eye out for predators at the expense of some other activity (e.g., foraging) and qualifies as an antipredator tactic. Obtain a copy of Bednekoff's (1997) paper entitled "Mutualism among safe, selfish sentinels: A dynamic game" (*American Naturalist*, vol. 150, pp. 373–392). Also obtain a copy of Wright et al.'s (2001) paper entitled "Safe selfish sentinels in a cooperative bird" (*Journal of Animal Ecology*, vol. 70, pp. 1070–1079). How do these two papers integrate what you learned in Chapter 9 (Cooperation) with concepts of antipredator behavior?

2. How does the example of the Dorset and Gwynedd minnows demonstrate important interactions between natural selection and learning in shaping antipredator behavior?

3. In the "Learning and Antipredator Behavior" section of the text, you were introduced to a series of studies by Alfieri, which examined how guppies benefit from associating with individuals that were predator-experienced. Indeed, naive guppies preferred to associate with experienced conspecifics. Why might animals benefit from associating with experienced animals? Also, construct several proximate hypotheses regarding *how* guppies might be able to distinguish between experienced and inexperienced groupmates.

4. Obtain a copy of Mirza et al.'s (2001) paper entitled "Differential responses of male and female red swordtails to chemical alarm cues" (*Journal of Fish Biology*, vol. 59, pp. 716–728). Discuss this paper in terms of: (1) proximate mechanisms involved in the detection of predation risk, and (2) within-population differences in antipredator behavior.

5. In 1973, Van Valen proposed what has been dubbed the "Red Queen hypothesis" which describes in part the evolutionary arms races that occur between predator and prey. This moniker was derived from Lewis Carrol's *Through the Looking Glass* in which the Red Queen says to Alice ". . . it takes all the running you can do to keep in the same place." The hypothesis says that both predator and prey are forced to evolve more complex hunting and antipredator tactics respectively, but neither can better its opponent. With this in mind, read Bergstrom and Lachmann's 2003 paper entitled "The Red King effect: When the slowest runner wins the coevolutionary race" (*Proceedings of the National Academy of Sciences, U.S.A.*, vol. 100, pp. 593–598). Contrast the Red Queen and the Red King effects in terms of: (1) the types of relationships that favor each effect, and (2) the rate of evolutionary change inherent in the arms race.

ANSWER KEY FOR MULTIPLE-CHOICE QUESTIONS

1.	d	6.	b
2.	c	7.	c
3.	e	8.	d
4.	e	9.	c
5.	a	10.	b

| Communication

DISCUSSION QUESTIONS

1. Bacteria often release chemicals that affect other bacteria in their vicinity. Would you consider this communication? If so, why? If not, would you consider the chemical trails that ants use to direct one another to a food source communication? How does that differ from the bacteria case, if at all?

Communication, as defined in this chapter, refers to the transfer of information from a signaler to a receiver. This definition is appealing because it makes no presumptions about the intentions of the individual emitting the signal or the individual receiving the signal, nor does it assume that all receivers were "targeted" recipients of the signal. Furthermore, this definition does not place limitations on the type of signal (e.g., broadcast vs. directed) transmitted between individuals, so long as at least one individual signals and at least one individual receives. Admittedly, it is difficult to envision how information might be conveyed between individual bacteria, but armed with our general definition of communication we can begin to answer this question. Anyone who has examined a bacterial culture under a light microscope would attest to the fact that bacterial populations can be colossal, thus the *potential* for interactions among individuals is likely to be quite high. Based on the opening sentence of this question, it is also clear that some individuals within these populations—signalers—emit chemical signals and that other individuals—receivers—are affected in some predictable way by coming into contact with this signal. Of course, the signal may not have been directed at any one individual per se, but for our purposes this doesn't really matter. Just as the chemical compounds secreted by leaf-cutter ants don't necessarily target any one individual, the chemical still qualifies as a signal that triggers changes in the behavior of ant receivers, presumably in response to some salient property of the compound. In both the bacteria and ant examples, emission of chemical compounds should be considered communication, particularly because these chemicals elicit modifications in receiver behavior.

If you are not yet convinced that chemical communication in bacteria might exist, consider the phenomenon of quorum sensing that has been discovered in myriad species of bacteria (from omnipresent *Agrobacterium* to deadly *Yersinia*). In a recent popular article, Michael Gross (2002) describes quorum sensing and some developments in the field of bacterial communication:

> The phenomenon was originally discovered in luminescent bacteria, which only light up when large numbers of them are around. In the 1970s, researchers showed that the bacteria secrete a molecular messenger, called the autoinducer, into the medium. They only produce light when they sense a threshold concentration of this molecule. For many years, biologists believed this communication to be specific to bioluminescence. It was only in the 1990s that they discovered quorum sensing to be a much more general phenomenon, involved in disparate processes including the synthesis of antibiotics in *Erwinia carotovora*, and the production of virulence factors in pathogenic bacteria.

The fact that bacteria communicate may be mind-blowing to some. But it is important to recognize that, just as bacteria respond to chemical signals with changes in physiology, gene expression, and so on, so too do animals, including humans. Physiological changes then precipitate a behavioral response, which at least for most is more easily identified in organisms that are larger than a fleck of dust! Nevertheless, the fact that these organisms cannot be seen without assistance does not preclude them from being able to communicate. If quorum sensing interests you, refer to some recent in-depth reviews on the topic (Miller and Bassler, 2001; Whitehead et al., 2001; Withers et al., 2001).

2. *One problem with examining whether a communication system more resembles exaggerations or "conspirational whispers" is that it is difficult to know how to define those terms for any given animal social system. How might you overcome this problem? Consider using a comparative study involving many related species.*

Krebs and Dawkins's manipulator/mind-reader scenario emphasizes the antagonistic aspects of signaling behavior—that is, the potential conflicts of interest that exist between signaler and receiver. In such systems, where cheating is a distinct possibility, costly signals may evolve as a result of an evolutionary arms race between signaler and receiver. In the words of Johnstone (1998):

> . . . the costly and conspicuous nature of many signals serves to enhance their reliability, by rendering it unprofitable for signalers to adopt a high level of display unless they are of high quality or in great need of a favorable response from the receiver. (p. 1554)

In contrast, when the interests of signaler and receiver coincide and the temptation to cheat does not exist, conspirational whispers should evolve so as to reduce the costs associated with communication. The question that arises is how we can distinguish between exaggerations and conspirational whispers. Because different animal systems employ different signaling tactics and because what constitutes an exaggerated signal for one species might qualify as a conspirational whisper for others, we are caught in somewhat of a dilemma. Nevertheless, by making comparisons among closely related species, we might be able to overcome this problem. How might we do this? First, we would have to identify taxa in which there exist substantial variation in the conspicuousness of a signal that serves the same general function in all species (e.g., color patterns and mate choice). Next, we would need to select species that occupy similar niches so as to eliminate the possibility that habitat differences drive differences in signal design. We would also need to control for any other factor that might influence signals such as color patterns. Last, we could develop a technique for measuring the fitness costs associated with color pattern variation in *each* species (e.g., energy, predation risk). It is important to note that, by converting qualitative measures of exaggeration (e.g., the color pattern *looks* bright or *appears* dull) to quantitative measures (e.g., probability of being eaten), we effectively eliminate subjectivity from our study.

Based on the above quote by Johnstone and the discussion of honesty and handicaps in the text, we might hypothesize that exaggerated signals (e.g., bright coloration patterns) are more costly to produce than conspirational whispers. Once the data on signal design and signal costs are collected for X number of species (which would be quite the arduous task), we could construct a graph that depicts the distribution of signal costs for all species. In an ideal world, we would obtain a bimodal distribution, with a peak in the "low-cost" range and a peak in the "high-cost" range, suggesting that some species utilize costly exaggerations, while others utilize relatively less costly whispers (with none in the middle). Of course, this type of experiment would be much more difficult to conduct in practice than has been described here, but the general logic presented here should at least get your intellectual wheels turning!

3. *Imagine you are studying a group of amphibian species that vary in their habitats, some living in dense, murky water, and others living in very clear ponds. What sorts of differences in communication systems would you expect to see across such species?*

The design of animal signals (e.g., modality, complexity, diversity) can be influenced by a number of different selection pressures, including the animals' social system, the sensory characteristics of signaler and receiver, and the habitat in which the animals live. To understand why we might expect differences in the communication systems of amphibian species living in dense, murky water versus clear ponds, we should first identify some features of the habitat that may constrain signal design—that is, features that make some signals more effective than others. To do this, we will focus on just a few habitat characteristics and touch on some of the many ways that such features could influence signal efficacy.

Dense habitats like forests or murky ponds can pose serious problems for the transmission of visual and acoustic signals. It is relatively easy to understand why the efficacy of visual signals might be reduced in murky ponds. Vegetation or debris could limit light levels or obstruct the visual field, both of which may diminish the effectiveness of visual signals (Endler, 1992). Complex habitats may also increase acoustic reverberation or attenuation, degradative alterations to sound that may limit the ability of receivers to perceive acoustic signals emitted by conspecifics. Electrical and mechanosensory signals may be influenced by dense habitats in similar ways as acoustic signals. Chemical signals, however, are less prone to bounce off of or be obstructed by vegetation or debris. Nevertheless, there are some constraints on the use of chemical signals—namely, the rate at which their effectiveness declines with dilution. Given these habitat constraints, we might expect natural selection to operate in ways that either favor different modes of communication across habitats or modify existing modes of communication in ways that increase signal transmission (Ord et al., 2002; Naguib, 2003).

With this (far from comprehensive) background, we are poised to make some predictions about how the communication systems of amphibians living in murky versus clear waters might differ. Let us assume, for the sake of simplicity, that these amphibian species have only visual and chemical signaling capabilities. Let us also assume that our amphibians communicate at close range and that the average distance over which signals must be transmitted is similar across species, regardless of habitat type. One simple prediction might be that species inhabiting murky waters should rely more heavily on chemical than visual communication. In habitats where visibility is low, visual signals degrade more rapidly and thus may be less effective or less reliable than chemical signals, even at close range. In addition, we might hypothesize that murky waters should favor more complex or conspicuous visual signals (e.g., large prominent color patches, increased display repetition) and that such exaggeration would be unnecessary for the transmission of information among individuals in the clear water habitats. Thus, murky water species should possess more elaborate visual signals than those that inhabit clear ponds. Our discussion has been biased toward characteristics of the signaler. Can you think of any ways in which the behavior or sensory physiology of the receivers might change as a function of the habitat?

4. *Suppose you are studying a heretofore unexamined species of primates. During your observations you note that individuals are often throwing heavy rocks against trees, causing a large "booming" sound. You speculate that individuals are communicating to one another using this technique. How might you go about testing this hypothesis?*

In this chapter, you encountered at least two examples where researchers documented what appeared to be interesting forms of communication (e.g., stridulation in leaf-cutter ants; color change in salmonids). Neither set of researchers, however, was satisfied with simply documenting the existence of a putative signal and concluding that communication was, indeed, at work. Rather, they took the extra step to determine whether another conspecific received the signal in question and whether receipt of the signal precipitated changes in receiver behavior. How does this relate to the question at hand? Being a keen observer (and listener), you document several instances of rock-throwing behavior in your primate population. At first, it is tempting to label this behavior as communication, just as was the case with ant stridulations and salmonid color changes. After all, why else would they spend the energy tossing gargantuan rocks against trees? Enticing as this hypothesis may be, we are lacking at least one critical piece of information—that is, whether any individuals respond to this booming signal. A plethora of possible explanations exist for how booming might function as a communicative signal. Do our primates throw rocks against trees to frighten potential predators? Do they boom to recruit conspecifics to prime feeding grounds? Could booming signal male quality—that is, the heavier the rock, the bigger the boom, the stronger the male? Along the same lines, might throwing rocks against trees help to preserve territorial boundaries? For the sake of argument, let us assume that we have reason to hypothesize that booming behavior is an intrasexual signal used by males to demonstrate physical prowess and that both territorial and nonterritorial males engage in this behavior. During our first field season, we document as many characteristics of our primate population as we can, including sex ratio, territory size, home range size, food distribution, individual territory status, the incidence of booming behavior, and the sound characteristics of each boom. In addition, we use a digital recorder to capture the booming sounds and add them to our computer. After hours of crunching through data files, we find some interesting trends: (1) nonterritorial males boom when approaching the territories of other males, (2) territorial males boom only when an intruder has been detected, (3) large males generally pick up larger rocks and therefore produce baritone booms, and (4) females, juveniles, and subadults do not engage in rock-tossing behavior. These data seem to suggest that rock throwing acts as some sort of territorial signal, but one important piece of data that we are lacking is whether territorial or nonterritorial males alter their behavior after hearing a boom. To address this question, we use the booms that were captured in the previous field season to fabricate some computer-generated booms of our own that cover a range of frequencies in the sound spectrum. We then purchase the most highly touted surround-sound speakers on the market and set out to our field site to conduct boom playback experiments. To execute this experiment, we first identify all territorial and nonterritorial males in the population and track their movement patterns such that we know where any given male is at any given time. We place speakers at various posts along the boundaries of each territorial males' territory. We then play one of three types of computer-generated booms—high, intermediate, or low frequency—to our territorial males and record their behavioral response to the booms. In addition, we locate nonterritorial males and project the same sets of booms into their general vicinity. After analyzing the data we find that territorial males: (1) respond to low-frequency booms by aggressively approaching the speakers and throwing rocks of their own, (2) respond to booms of intermediate frequency by approaching the speaker, (3) do not exhibit any observable changes in behavior in response to high-frequency booms. The exact opposite trend was found for nonterritorial males (there was more pronounced approach behavior toward high-frequency booms). The data from our second season clearly demonstrate that throwing rocks against trees qualifies as a form of communication in our primate population. Booms produced by a signaler elicit specific behavioral responses from receivers, and the type of response depends both on the quality (frequency) of the signal and the identity of the receiver (territorial vs. nonterritorial). Based on these results, can you come up with a hypothesis to explain why territorial and nonterritorial males exhibit differential responses to the booms?

MULTIPLE-CHOICE QUESTIONS

1. Which of the following is required for communication to occur?
   a. The signaler and receiver must be in very close proximity to one another.
   b. The signaler and receiver must be conspecifics.
   c. Signals must be directed at a particular receiver.
   d. There must be at least one signaler and one receiver.
   e. Visual cues must be used in tandem with chemical, auditory, or vibrational cues.

2. Which component of the honeybee waggle dance provides information about the distance to a resource?
   a. length of the dance
   b. number of pauses contained within the dance
   c. angle at which the honeybee orients during the dance
   d. amount of physical contact the dancer makes with other hive members
   e. release of pheromones during the dance

3. A play marker indicates that a certain behavior
   a. is too costly to exhibit during play.
   b. was unexpectedly fierce.
   c. will not be used during subsequent bouts of play.
   d. cannot be used during play.
   e. is exhibited in a playful context.

4. The classical ethological approach to communication posits that
   a. both the signaler and the receiver benefit from information exchange and that there is little selection pressure favoring deceitful communication.
   b. signaling exchanges represent evolutionary arms races between signalers and receivers.
   c. honest signaling cannot evolve in the context of animal communication.
   d. neither the signaler nor the receiver benefit from information exchange, thus leading to the elimination of communication altogether.
   e. even if selection pressures favor dishonest communication, signalers and receivers will never engage in deceitful signaling.

5. Leaf-cutter ants use _____ for long-range communication and use _____ for close-range communication.
   a. visual displays; pheromones
   b. stridulations; visual displays
   c. pheromones; stridulations
   d. visual displays; electrical impulses
   e. pheromones; pheromones

6. Which of the following statements concerning birdsong is *true*?
   a. Birds have several different vocal organs, which they use for different songs.
   b. Some birds can operate both sides of the syrinx independently throughout their song without one side being dominant.
   c. Neither side of the avian syrinx can dominate certain frequencies used in song production.
   d. Respiratory muscles that supply air to the syrinx play no part in song output.
   e. The avian syrinx has three compartments, which can be used to emit different types of sound.

7. Cooperative signaling should favor the evolution of
   a. increased energetic investment in signal design.
   b. exaggerated displays.
   c. conspirational whispers.
   d. deceitful signaling tactics.
   e. communication breakdown.

8. According to the handicap principle, honest signaling can evolve if traits involved in communication
   a. are very costly to fake.
   b. are fairly easy to produce.
   c. are used for many forms of communication.
   d. are impossible to produce.
   e. are beneficial to the signaler.

9. Which of the following statements provides preliminary evidence that whale coda dialects could arise via social learning?
   a. Very little genetic variation and coda variation exist between groups.
   b. Variation in coda dialects is greater within groups than between groups.
   c. Substantial genetic variation exists between groups.
   d. Individuals communicate using the codas of the group into which they were born, rather than the codas of the group that they currently occupy.
   e. Between-group coda variation is greater than within-group coda variation, and individuals within groups sing similar codas for extended periods of time.

10. Deceptive or dishonest signaling will provide the greatest benefit when
    a. cooperative signalers are rare compared to dishonest signalers.
    b. individuals signal honestly half the time and dishonestly half the time.
    c. dishonest signalers have no stake in the outcome.
    d. cooperative signalers and dishonest signalers are equally common.
    e. dishonest signalers are rare compared to cooperative signalers.

REVIEW AND CHALLENGE QUESTIONS

1. Describe the primary differences between Dawkins and Krebs's (1978) view of communication and the classical ethological approach.

2. How does Zahavi's handicap principle apply to signaler-receiver dynamics? What are Zahavi's most critical assumptions?

3. As described in the chapter, animals may use many signaling modalities to communicate information to conspecifics—that is, signals may be visual, chemical, electrical, acoustic, or vibratory. Imagine that you are studying signaler-receiver behavior in the context of aggressive disputes in a certain species of fish known to use visual, chemical, and acoustic cues during contests. Design a series of experiments that would allow you to tease apart the relative contribution of these different signaling modalities to the dynamics of aggressive contests in these fish.

4. Obtain a copy of McGregor and Peake's (2000) article entitled "Communication networks: Social environments for receiving and signalling behavior" (*Acta Ethologica*, vol. 2, pp. 71–81). In what ways is the communication network concept fundamentally different from the traditional view that communication occurs between a signaler-receiver dyad? Can you think of any types of signaler-receiver interactions, aside from those covered in the article, that could be amenable to interpretation using the communication networks concept?

5. The vast majority of this chapter focused on intraspecific communication. Do you think communication occurs between individuals of different species?

To assist in your quest to understand interspecific communication, consider Schuett and his colleagues' 1984 paper "Feeding mimicry in the rattlesnake *Sistrurus catenatus*, with comment on the evolution of the rattle" (*Animal Behavior*, vol. 32, pp. 625–626), in which they describe a form of feeding mimicry in juvenile rattlesnakes called caudal luring. Do you think caudal luring qualifies as a form of communication? If so, would you consider this type of rattlesnake behavior to be deceitful signaling? If not, provide support for your answer.

ANSWER KEY FOR MULTIPLE-CHOICE QUESTIONS

1.	d	6.	b
2.	a	7.	c
3.	e	8.	a
4.	a	9.	e
5.	c	10.	e

| # Habitat Selection, Territoriality, and Migration

DISCUSSION QUESTIONS

1. *Make a general list of the costs and benefits of territoriality. Using that list, determine what sort of environments would generally favor the formation of long-term territories.*

When animals occupy particular areas and defend these areas against conspecific competitors, they are said to be **territorial**. To understand why animals establish territories or to understand why territories are structured in certain ways (e.g., size), ethologists examine the benefits and costs of territorial behavior. Some of the benefits to territoriality include gaining exclusive access to food resources, shelter, and reproductive opportunity. But with the benefits come substantial costs in the form of territorial defense. To maintain a territory, the owner must expend considerable energy in defense against rivals that attempt to usurp "rights" to the area. If the territory owner is constantly chasing away competitors, it necessarily loses time that could have been spent feeding, courting a mate, or remaining vigilant for predation threats (on the territory owner itself or the territory owner's offspring). These types of costs are generally classified as opportunity costs—that is, the territory owner loses the *opportunity* to conduct other fitness-related activities when defending the territory. Costs associated with meeting the energetic demands of territorial defense could also be manifest as a general decline in health, including complications such as suppression of the immune system. As described in the chapter, dear enemy effects may reduce the costs of territorial defense.

Now that the general costs and benefits have been outlined, we turn to the question at hand: what sort of environments would favor the formation of long-term territories? The simple answer to this question is that long-term territoriality will be favored in environments where the benefits gained as a territory holder outweigh the costs sustained in defense for an extended period of time. For instance, if food resources are unpredictably or patchily distributed or if there are substantial temporal changes in the availability of food (e.g., in seasonal environments), long-term territories would not be favored. Why? Because if a territory owner must not only defend its territory but also search far and wide for food, then defense and searching costs will likely exceed the benefits of obtaining sparsely distributed morsels. By the same token, if depleted resources on the territory are not renewable, the quality of the territory (and thus, the benefits of maintaining the territory) decrease relative to defense costs over time. Here again, it would not pay to establish a long-term territory.

2. The ideal free distribution model predicts that animals will distribute themselves among patches in proportion to resources. What sort of cognitive abilities, if any, does this assume on the part of animals? Would bacteria potentially distribute themselves in accordance with the predictions of IFD models?

In their simplest form, **ideal free distribution** models postulate that animals should occupy available habitats that are most profitable. The evolutionarily stable strategy for the IFD model states that animals should be distributed among accessible patches in proportion to the resources available in these patches. In addition, when the IFD equilibrium is achieved, all individuals have equal fitness, provided that everyone stays put (Maynard Smith, 1976). The question, then, is whether any sort of cognition is required for animals to achieve ideal free distribution. Based on the description in the "The Ideal Free Distribution Model and Habitat Choice" section of the text, animals simply need to gauge their returns in each patch, move from patch to patch occasionally to update patch quality information and choose the patch that provides the highest rate of intake. Animals can gauge habitat profitability in a number of ways, and their "decision" to move from one area to the next might be based on physiological responses to hunger, lack of nutrition, and so on. Thus, cognitive abilities are not a prerequisite for achieving the ideal free distribution equilibrium. As follows, bacteria should be expected to distribute themselves in accordance with IFD predictions if they have some mechanism with which to assess patch quality (or their own returns in any given patch) and relocate. Nevertheless, this is not to say that some level of cognition cannot be involved in attaining the IFD. Recent empirical and theoretical work has incorporated individual learning, limits on the ability of animals to perceive differences between habitats (Beauchamp et al., 1997; Collins et al., 2002; Koops and Abrahams, 2003), and observational learning (Koops and Abrahams, 1999) to either elaborate on the IFD model or to explain cases where the IFD model is not unequivocally met (e.g., when animals exploit poor patches more than expected).

3. Suppose that young individuals watch older conspecifics choose their territories and subsequently use such information in their habit-choice decisions about valu-

able resources. Outline one scenario by which such observational learning could increase competition for prime habitat sites, and one in which it would decrease competition for such sites.

As described in the "Territoriality" section of this chapter, individuals may pay attention to territorial settlement decisions of conspecifics. Observing the territorial decisions of others may influence the behavior of animals that have not yet established, or are in the process of establishing, a territory of their own (e.g., conspecific cueing hypothesis). Provided that the presence of individuals on a territory indicates something about territory quality, we might expect the observers to search for territories with similar characteristics as those that other individuals already occupy (e.g., temperature, predation threat, available cover, presence of nutritious food resources). Thus, observational learning may decrease the variability in what is considered to be a favorable territory. When could observational learning—in this case, learning about the characteristics of quality territories by observing others—increase or decrease competition for prime territories?

Let us assume that picking a prime territory takes some practice—that is, inexperienced animals are more likely to choose mediocre territories than experienced animals. Also, let us assume that mediocre territories are more abundant than prime territories. Now, imagine a scenario in which inexperienced animals were first to establish territories. If observers copied the territory choice of these untested individuals, and if such territories were abundant, then competition among putative territory owners would probably be negligible. What would happen if experienced animals were first to establish territories? In this case, experienced animals would occupy territories that were both high in quality and limited in number. If observers copied the habitats chosen by others, and if such territories were few and far between, then competition among territory owners might be intense. Thus, depending on the experience of the initial territory holders, observational learning could either increase or decrease competition for available sites.

4. *In the literature on "sneaker" and "parental" male bluegill sunfish there has been some debate as to whether there are distinct genetic morphs—that is, genes encoding each strategy—or whether each individual is capable of becoming either a sneaker or a parental male, and uses environmental or social cues to make this decision. Can you sketch out an experiment to distinguish between these hypotheses?*

Animal systems in which sneaker and parental phenotypes exist are a fascinating example of how **alternative male reproductive tactics** can be maintained in a population (Taborsky, 1994; Gross, 1996; Moczek and Emlen, 2000). Whether these alternative phenotypes have a genetic or nongenetic basis (e.g., ontogenetic, social, or environmental) remains an interesting question among ethologists. If sneaker and parental phenotypes have a genetic basis, then: (1) animals that exhibit either strategy should do so throughout their entire life, and (2) the phenotype may be inherited (Ryan and Rosenthal, 2001; see "Ruff Satellites" section of Chapter 17). But a host of nongenetic factors may also trigger changes in the reproductive tactics a male adopts. A classic ontogenetic example involves body size, which often correlates well with age in fish. Young, small males cannot compete with older, large males for access to females. Thus, small males adopt sneaking tactics, while large males defend territories. Another possibility is that males assume certain reproductive strategies based not on absolute size (or age) but on their size relative to other males in their social group. Here, the strategy that an animal adopts depends more on social cues. In either case, the males exhibit phenotypic plasticity—that is, phenotypes can change based on a host of environmental or social conditions. If sneaker and parental phenotypes have an ontogenetic or social basis, then: (1) animals may change their strategy depending either on their absolute size/age or their size relative to others in the social group, and (2) specific phenotypes should not be inherited (but, the ability to switch tactics may very well be).

Observational studies that track the reproductive behavior of males throughout their lives may be a starting point for determining whether "sneaker" and "parental" phenotypes are genetically or environmentally determined. In addition, experiments that manipulate the social milieu (e.g., transferring the smallest male of one group to a group composed of even smaller individuals) will also provide insights into whether the males can switch their reproductive strategies when placed in different environmental or social conditions. If observational and experimental studies yield no evidence for phenotypic plasticity, the next step might be to conduct experiments aimed at estimating heritability of the trait in question (e.g., size, strategy; see Chapter 2).

5. Consider Møller and Erritzøe's work on immune defense organs and migration behavior. Can you make any predictions regarding how a migrating species might fare against local parasites (in both its habitats) as compared to resident species? What is the logic underlying your hypothesis?

Møller and Erritzøe's (1998) study demonstrated that migratory species invest more in organs related to immune defense (bursa of Fabricus and spleen) than closely related nonmigratory species. These results make intuitive sense in that the migratory species may be exposed to a wider variety of parasites and pathogens (some from each environment) than nonmigratory species and thus should be prepared to mount a greater immune response. The above question is concerned with whether increased investment in immune defense organs allows migratory species to be as *efficient* at tackling infection in each environment as nonmigratory species that are constantly exposed to the same set of infectious agents. One plausible answer is provided below, but this answer should be considered as only one of many possible alternatives.

Let us assume, as is likely the case, that it is energetically costly to mount an immune response (e.g., manufacturing antibodies, mobilizing T-cells and macrophages, producing memory cells that aid in the secondary immune response, increasing spleen size). Let us also assume that any given animal can contribute only a finite amount of energy to the immune response without compromising other activities such as reproduction—that is, a tradeoff exists. If both of these assumptions are true, migratory species may be less efficient at overcoming infection by local parasites in either of the two habitats (e.g., winter feeding grounds and summer breeding grounds) than their nonmigratory counterparts. The logic underlying this hypothesis is that nonmigratory species can dedicate their full energy allotment to mounting a defense against a specific set of local parasites, while migratory species need to partition this energy allotment to resist parasitic infection from two sets of local parasites (particularly if parasites linger with the migratory species even after migration has commenced).

MULTIPLE-CHOICE QUESTIONS

1. Which of the following prediction(s) arise from the ideal free distribution model?
   a. Distribution of individuals matches the distribution of competitors across patches.
   b. At equilibrium, individuals that stay put will obtain fewer resources than those that move between patches.
   c. At equilibrium, moving to a new patch yields more resources.
   d. Habitat choice decisions should be based on the decisions of others.
   e. Distribution of individuals matches the distribution of resources across patches.

2. Of the following conditions, which one favors staying on a territory to help raise young?
   a. Available territories are abundant.
   b. Breeding opportunities outside the natal territory are scarce.
   c. Breeding opportunities outside the natal territory are abundant.
   d. Few competitors exist outside the natal territory.
   e. The helper is distantly related, or unrelated, to the young.

3. Abiotic factors that can influence the habitat an animal chooses include
   a. availability and location of mates.
   b. distribution of prey items.
   c. distribution of putative predators.
   d. parasite density.
   e. availability of shelter.

4. In its simplest form, the conspecific cueing hypothesis examines whether
   a. animals learn about the characteristics of a territory from their interactions with other individuals.
   b. animals actively communicate information about territory quality to one another.
   c. juveniles acquire information about how to properly defend territories by watching their parents.
   d. females prefer to mate with males that occupy superior territories.
   e. animals learn about the relative quality of many territories by comparing the health of the individuals occupying those areas.

5. Males that do not establish a territory of their own, but rather are sometimes tolerated on a territorial male's residence in exchange for assistance in territorial defense are referred to as
   a. sneakers.
   b. streakers.
   c. satellites.
   d. bourgeois.
   e. mimics.

6. Irruptive migration refers to a situation in which
   a. annual migration is obligatory.
   b. millions of animals migrate at the same time.
   c. migration occurs only when conditions are poor.
   d. animals migrate over distances that exceed 3,000 kilometers.
   e. certain species migrate multiple times during the same year.

7. An individual that adopts a dear enemy strategy
   a. constantly renegotiates territorial boundaries with its neighbor.
   b. remains vigilant against its neighbor on the assumption that it cannot be trusted.
   c. does not challenge its neighbor over territorial boundaries.
   d. allows satellite males to settle on its neighbor's territory, but not its own.
   e. b and c

8. Which of the following factors has *not* been implicated as a means by which fish migrate back to their natal stream as adults?
   a. magnetic compass
   b. food availability
   c. learning via exposure to chemical cues
   d. celestial cues
   e. drifting currents

9. If the ideal free distribution is achieved, then individuals that move from the patch they currently occupy will
   a. gain significantly more access to resources.

b. be punished by individuals from the patch that they left.

c. not be able to enter a new patch until the next breeding season.

d. migrate to an area with less predation risk.

e. suffer reduced payoffs relative to individuals that stay put.

10. Getty's defensive coalition game employs which of the following models to examine coalition formation among neighboring territory holders?

a. prisoner's dilemma

b. polygyny threshold

c. group selection

d. inclusive fitness

e. reproductive skew

REVIEW AND CHALLENGE QUESTIONS

1. Suppose you are studying alternative reproductive tactics in male beetles, and you find that small, sneaker males enjoy similar lifetime reproductive success as large, territorial males. You also find that large males always defeat small males in head-to-head combat and that female beetles prefer to mate with large males. How do you suppose that small, sneaker males have equal reproductive success to that of large, territorial males?

2. Describe the primary difference between a territory and a home range.

3. Under what environmental circumstances do you think it would be advantageous to forego a territorial lifestyle in favor of living in groups?

4. What type of information is important for a territorial animal to learn before versus after territorial establishment?

5. Why is the relationship between territory holders and satellites sometimes considered to be a case of conditional cooperation? Under what circumstances will this cooperative interaction break down?

ANSWER KEY FOR MULTIPLE-CHOICE QUESTIONS

1.	e	6.	c
2.	b	7.	c
3.	e	8.	b
4.	a	9.	e
5.	c	10.	a

CHAPTER 14 | Aggression

DISCUSSION QUESTIONS

1. In 1990, Enquist and Leimar published a paper, "The evolution of fatal fighting" (Animal Behaviour, 39, 1–9). When do you think fighting to the death might evolve?

Enquist and Leimar investigated the evolution of fatal fighting strategies in their 1990 *Animal Behaviour* paper. Intuitively, one might think that animals should be able to settle their differences without engaging in lethal combat. But Enquist and Leimar provided several examples of fatal fights, particularly in insects and arachnids (see also Cook et al., 1999; Cushing and Reese, 1999; West et al., 2001; Bean and Cook, 2002; Anderson et al., 2003). The question then becomes: What conditions will favor animals that fight to the death? The mathematical analysis conducted by Enquist and Leimar suggests that fatal fighting strategies will evolve when the value of the current resource exceeds the value of future resources. In other words, if an animal is not liable to obtain resources of much value in the future, it should fight vigorously (and often to the death) for the current contested resource. Enquist and Leimar denoted the current resource value as V and the expected future resource value as V_0. In Figure 3 of their paper, they showed that as the ratio of V_0/V decreases—that is, the current resource value is greater than the expected future resource value—the probability of fatal fighting increases dramatically. When V_0/V drops below 0.5, fatal fights are almost certain to occur.

The general conclusion is that fatal fights will evolve when the value of future resources is particularly low relative to the current contested resource. A typical example involving mating success appears in the discussion section of Enquist and Leimar. Imagine a species characterized by a short life span and in which females mate only once. If a male encounters a receptive female late in the breeding season (or toward the waning stages of his life), the value (V) of mating with this female is exceptionally high, particularly if the male has not yet mated. In addition, the prospect that this male will obtain future mates is bleak—that is, V_0 is low—given that it is late in the reproductive season. Thus, this male should be willing to exhibit escalatory and even fatal fighting tactics to obtain access to the receptive female.

2. *The classic hawk-dove game we examined in this chapter assumes that losers pay a cost (C) that is not paid by winners. In the matrix below, we are assuming that both hawks in a fight pay a cost. For the case of both V > C and V < C, calculate the ESS for this new game.*

	Hawk	Dove
Hawk	$V/2 - C$	V
Dove	0	$V/2$

To answer this question, let us revisit some important definitions. An individual that plays the hawk strategy escalates during a contest—that is, uses fighting tactics other than display—and continues to escalate until it is injured or until its opponent gives up. An individual that plays the dove strategy displays during a contest but gives up if its opponent escalates. An **evolutionarily stable strategy (ESS)**, as described in Chapter 9 (Math Box 9.1), is defined as "a strategy such that, if all the members of a population adopt it, no mutant strategy can invade" (Maynard Smith, 1982); a mutant strategy refers to a new strategy that enters the population. Strategies will be evolutionarily stable if the payoff of adopting that strategy exceeds the payoff of adopting mutant strategies. Now, let us examine the above matrix to see whether hawk (H) or dove (D) is an ESS.

a. Is dove an ESS? In other words, can a population full of doves resist invasion by new, mutant hawk strategies? Using the logic provided in Math Box 9.1, we can ask two questions. First, does the expected payoff that doves receive when contesting with other doves exceed the payoff that hawks receive when contesting with doves? More formally, is E (D, D) > E (H, D)? Given that E (D, D) = V/2 and E (H, D) = V, the question becomes, is V/2 > V? No! Under no circumstance can half of the resource value exceed the full resource value. Thus, dove is not an ESS. Notice that the cost (C) does not matter in calculating whether dove is an ESS. Thus, regardless of whether V > C or C > V, doves will be unable to resist invasion by new, mutant hawk strategies.

b. Is hawk an ESS? In other words, can a population full of hawks resist invasion by new, mutant dove strategies? Using the logic provided in Math Box 9.1, we can ask two questions. First, does the expected payoff that hawks receive when contesting with other hawks exceed the payoff that doves receive when contesting with hawks? More formally, is E (H, H) > E (D, H)? Given that E (H, H) = (V/2) – C and E (D, H) = 0, is (V/2) – C > 0? The answer to this question is that it depends on the relationship between V and C! To demonstrate this point, examine the following table:

Condition	Result (V/2) – C = ?	Is (V/2) – C > 0?
V = C, where V = 1, C = 1	(V/2) – C= (1/2) – 1 = –1/2	No, (V/2) – C < 0
V < C, where V = 1, C = 2	(V/2) – C = (1/2) – 2 = –3/2	No, (V/2) – C < 0
V < C, where V = 1, C = 3	(V/2) – C = (1/2) – 3 = –5/2	No, (V/2) – C < 0
V > C, where V = 2, C = 1	(V/2) – C = (2/2) – 1 = 0	No, (V/2) – C = 0
V > C, where V = 3, C = 1	(V/2) – C = (3/2) – 1 = 1/2	Yes, (V/2) – C > 0

By examining the table above, you should see that (V/2) – C > 0 only when the value of the resource is more than twice the cost of engaging in a fight. When V < 2C, hawk is not an ESS because (V/2) – C is not greater than 0. However, depending on the degree to which resource value (V) exceeds contest costs (C), hawk could be an ESS.

We are left with somewhat of a dilemma for all circumstances where the value of the resource is not at least twice the cost of fighting. Here, neither hawk nor dove is evolutionarily stable. The next question that we can ask is whether some mixture of hawks and doves constitutes an ESS (see Math Box 14.1). The **equilibrium frequency** of hawks and doves refers to the condition under which the payoff to hawks is equal to the payoff for doves. To calculate this equilibrium frequency, denote p as the proportion of hawks in the population and $(1 – p)$ as the proportion of doves.

The overall payoff for hawks is as follows: $p[(V/2) – C] + (1 – p)V$. That is, a certain proportion of the time (p), hawks will encounter other hawks and experience a payoff of $(V/2)$ – C. The remainder of the time $(1 – p)$, hawks will encounter doves and experience a payoff of V. Adding these two payoffs together provides the overall payoff for hawks.

The overall payoff for doves is as follows: $p(0) + (1 – p)(V/2)$. That is, a certain proportion of the time (p), doves will encounter hawks and experience a payoff of 0. The remainder of the time $(1 – p)$, doves will encounter other doves and experience a payoff of V/2. Adding these two payoffs together provides the overall payoff for doves.

When does the payoff to hawks equal the payoff to doves? This requires some simple algebra:

Step 1: $p[(V/2) – C] + (1 – p)V = p(0) + (1 – p)(V/2)$
Step 2: $pV/2 – pC + V – pV = V/2 – pV/2$
Subtract V/2 from both sides of the equation to yield
Step 3: $pV/2 – pC + V/2 – pV = –pV/2$

Step 4: $pV - pC + V/2 - pV = 0$
Step 5: $-pC + V/2 = 0$
Step 6: $-pC = -V/2$
Step 7: $p = V/2C$

Thus, the equilibrium frequency occurs when the proportion of hawks in the population is equal to V/2C and the proportion of doves in the population is equal to (1 – V/2C). This equilibrium frequency could also be interpreted as follows: each individual in the population will play hawk with probability V/2C and dove with probability (1 – V/2C) (see Chapter 17 introduction for more on this).

The major conclusions of this ESS analysis are as follows:

a. Dove alone can never be an ESS under the conditions described in the original matrix.

b. Hawk alone cannot be an ESS when V < 2C.

c. Hawk is evolutionarily stable when the value of the contested resource is *at least* twice the cost of fighting (when V ≥ 2C).

d. When V < 2C both hawks and doves can be maintained in the population with an equilibrium frequency of V/2C and (1 – V/2C) respectively.

3. *A number of studies have suggested that loser effects are both more common and more dramatic than winner effects. Construct a hypothesis as to why this might be. How could you test your hypothesis?*

Losers of aggressive contests are often less likely to initiate future fights and to win these fights—that is, they show the loser effect. In contrast, winners of aggressive contests are often more likely to initiate subsequent encounters and to win these fights—that is, they show the winner effect. As described in the text, loser effects are often more pronounced than winner effects and, in some species, winner effects are absent altogether. The reasons for this difference between loser and winner effects continue to elude researchers and, to date, no empirical studies have examined, in detail, the underlying reasons for this difference. Thus, the following answer should be considered just one of many possible alternatives.

Hypothesis: It is more costly to engage in future interactions following a loss than following a win, although winners that initiate future interactions also experience non-negligible costs. Thus, it is costly to start fights, but particularly so as a loser. This hypothesis concentrates on the costs of future aggressive interactions. To test this hypothesis, you would need to establish that (1) it is more costly for losers to engage in future contests than it is for winners to do the same (e.g., effects on reproductive opportunity, physiology), (2) differences in the persistence or magnitude of winner and loser effects exist, and (3) discrepancies between winners and losers in the costs of starting future fights are causally linked to the persistence and magnitude of winner and loser effects.

4. *If stress-related hormones such as cortisol often inhibit learning and/or memory, how might that compound the difficulties subordinate fish face in trying to raise their rank in hierarchies?*

As described in the text, subordinate animals often experience elevated stress hormone levels that have been implicated as having a negative effect on learning and memory (for alternatives, see Shors, 2001; Roozendaal, 2002). How could impaired learning or memory be of further detriment to subordinate animals in terms of the prospects for increased rank? One of many possible scenarios where subordinate status, stress hormones, and learning interact to impede future increases in rank is described here.

An animal's dominance rank depends on its competitive ability: individuals that are less competitively adept usually rank lower in the dominance hierarchy. Size is a major determinant of competitive success, and growth relies on the utilization of efficient foraging tactics. Learning where the most profitable food patches are located and retaining this information are likely to be crucial for obtaining food, growing, and gaining a competitive advantage. Increased stress hormone levels in subordinate animals might impair their ability to relocate lucrative foraging sites and could thus limit their growth rate. This, in turn, could limit their size and ability to compete for dominance rank with well-fed, larger group members. Of course, a suite of alternatives could be devised for how stress hormones and learning impairment affect subordinate animals' opportunity to increase rank. Developing hypotheses marks only the beginning of the scientific process in animal behavior (or any other field). Thus, ideas such as the one provided above should not be taken at face value, but rather, they should be subject to rigorous experimental testing before any conclusions are drawn.

MULTIPLE-CHOICE QUESTIONS

1. Which two variables are common to all game theory models of aggressive contests?
   a. resource value and territory size
   b. relatedness and ownership
   c. contest costs and resource value
   d. territory size and relatedness
   e. ownership and contest costs

2. Which of the following answers best describes the ESS for the hawk-dove game when $V > C$; $V < C$?
   a. Dove is the only ESS; dove is the only ESS.
   b. Equilibrium frequency of hawks and doves; hawk is the only ESS.
   c. Hawk is the only ESS; hawk is the only ESS.
   d. Hawk is the only ESS; equilibrium frequency of hawks and doves.
   e. Dove is the only ESS; equilibrium frequency of hawks and doves.

3. Which of the following is *not* a key prediction of the sequential assessment game?
   a. Contests are characterized by a series of increasingly escalated bouts.
   b. Repeating signals within each bout decreases random error and increases assessment accuracy.
   c. Contests should begin with the least dangerous behavior.
   d. Contests between well-matched opponents should be longer than contests between individuals that differ considerably in fighting ability.
   e. The costs of fighting are minimal.

4. Animals that adopt antibourgeois strategies
   a. play hawk p proportion of the time and dove $1 - p$ proportion of the time, regardless of territorial status.
   b. play hawk when owner, dove when intruder.
   c. play dove when occupying high-quality territories, dove when occupying low-quality territories.
   d. play dove when owner, hawk when intruder.
   e. play dove when occupying high-quality territories, hawk when occupying low-quality territories.

5. In a group of four individuals (A, B, C, and D), a linear hierarchy emerges when
   a. A beats B and C; B beats C and D; C beats D; D beats A.
   b. A beats B, C, and D; B beats D; C beats B and D; D beats no one.
   c. A beats B, C, and D; B beats C; C beats D; D beats B.
   d. A beats B; B beats C and D; C beats A and D; D beats A.
   e. A beats B, C, and D; B beats C and D; C beats D; D beats no one.

6. Which of the following assumptions/predictions apply to the war of attrition model:
   a. Contest costs are substantial.
   b. The strategy set is discrete rather than continuous.
   c. There is an evolutionarily stable distribution of contest lengths.
   d. Cues such as size and ownership can be used to settle a contest.
   e. a and c

7. Bystander effects occur when
   a. winning a contest increases the probability of winning future contests.
   b. the observer of an interaction changes its assessment of the fighting abilities of those that it observed.
   c. individuals change their fighting behavior if they are watched.
   d. losing a contest decreases that probability of winning future contests.
   e. bystanders actively interfere with the aggressive interactions between two conspecifics.

8. One of the most important aspects of Hsu and Wolf's study on winner and loser effects in *Rivulus marmoratus* was that
   a. winner effects were significantly stronger than loser effects.
   b. previous winners experience an increased probability of winning against previous losers but not against inexperienced opponents.
   c. fighting experiences obtained in the distant past explained close to all of the variation in current winning probabilities.
   d. the probability of winning future fights depended only on an animal's most recent fighting experience.
   e. both an animal's most recent and "next to last" experiences affected future contest success, with recent experiences being more influential.

9. Which of the following statements regarding the effects of serotonin on aggressive behavior is *true*?
   a. Increased serotonergic function is correlated with increased aggression in crustaceans.
   b. Serotonin elicits the same profile of aggressive behavior across all taxa.
   c. Low social status decreases serotonergic activity in Atlantic charr.
   d. Serotonin is not involved in the expression of aggressive behavior in mammals.
   e. Hierarchy status is the only type of social and/or environmental stimulus that elicits changes in serotonergic activity in animals.

10. Schuett's research on corticosterone and fighting in copperhead snakes (*Agkistrodon contortrix*) demonstrated that
    a. losing males do not court available females.
    b. plasma corticosterone levels were significantly greater in losers than in winners or controls.
    c. losing males rarely challenged other males.
    d. circulating corticosterone levels were not influenced by contest length.
    e. all of the above

REVIEW AND CHALLENGE QUESTIONS

1. Do you think past fighting experience affects social animals in the same manner as it affects solitary animals? Provide a hypothesis that addresses why winning or losing experiences would have the same (or different) effects on solitary versus social animals.

2. Describe several key differences between the hawk-dove and war of attrition game theory models.

3. What conditions should favor animals that adopt antibourgeois strategies? What conditions should favor animals that adopt bourgeois strategies?

4. Why would some animals in a population opt to observe aggressive contests rather than engage in actual physical combat? In other words, under what conditions will watching fights between others be advantageous?

5. This chapter describes bystander effects as situations in which bystanders change their estimation of the fighting ability of individuals they *observe* fighting. Do you think information other than that provided by visual cues is available to a bystander? Also, based on previous chapters, do you think bystander effects could operate in other social contexts?

6. Steroid hormones (e.g., testosterone, corticosterone) are certainly involved in aggressive disputes in many animals. However, are steroid hormone levels the *cause* or the *consequence* of aggressive interactions? For instance, do animals with high testosterone levels become dominant or does dominance status result in elevated testosterone levels? Devise an experiment to test these two alternatives (for a hint, see "Communication Venues—A Shocking Example of Mate Choice" in Chapter 12).

ANSWER KEY FOR MULTIPLE-CHOICE QUESTIONS

1.	c	6.	c
2.	d	7.	b
3.	e	8.	e
4.	d	9.	a
5.	e	10.	e

CHAPTER 15

Play

DISCUSSION QUESTIONS

1. Based on what you have learned in this chapter, try to construct a definition of play. After you have done so, answer the following questions: Does your definition cover all cases of play? Does it cover behavior that you don't consider to be play?

The primary objective of this question is to have you develop your own definition of play and polish your definition by considering both its specificity and its general applicability to animal behavior. This may best be accomplished by coordinating conferences and debate sessions with your classmates. With this being said, any number of definitions could potentially be provided for you, but doing so would render this answer a reference rather than a teaching tool. To help you get started, let us first revisit the definition provided in the text and then outline some questions that you may want to consider in constructing your own definition of play.

Despite the nebulous qualities of **play**, Bekoff and Byers (1981) have formulated a useful definition: "Play is all motor activity performed postnatally that appears to be purposeless, in which motor patterns from other contexts may often be used in modified forms and altered temporal sequencing." Nonetheless, even this definition has drawbacks: First, it is descriptive rather than functional in nature. Second, adhering to this definition might lead us to categorize some types of behavior as play when, intuitively speaking, they do not appear to be play (e.g., pacing of zoo animals, repeated blinking of one's eyes). Based on the pros and cons of Bekoff and Byers's definition, how can you go about constructing a viable definition of your own? Just as animals must fine-tune their recognition templates so as to avoid rejecting kin (or accepting nonkin; see the answer to Discussion Question 1 in Chapter 8), you should weigh the benefits of providing a *specific* definition for play against the costs of developing a *general* definition. On the one hand, if your definition is too general, you run the risk of including behaviors that most would not consider play (acceptance errors). On the other hand, if your definition is too specific, you run the risk of excluding behaviors that most would actually consider play (rejection errors). With this in mind, here are some questions that may help you to construct a workable definition for play:

a. Should your definition focus on the structure or function of play (contrast Bekoff and Byers, 1981, and Spinka et al., 2001)? Or should your definition provide a happy medium between structure and function?

b. What exactly is play behavior directed at: inanimate objects, conspecifics, or neither?

c. What are the fitness costs and benefits associated with play?

d. Are some types of motor patterns more characteristic of play than others?

Clearly, there are many more questions that you and your classmates can entertain in formulating a definition of play. But the above questions and considerations should assist you in developing a feasible definition. Given the current "I know it when I see it" definitions, you are almost sure to provide some insights into the study of play behavior in animals.

2. In the interview, Bernd Heinrich argues that we can never know whether play is enjoyable to nonhumans. Can you construct an argument that it is, at least in principle, possible to know the answer to this question? If so, what would your argument be? If not, can you give other reasons beside those covered by Heinrich that explain why you believe we can't know whether animals enjoy play?

In our quest to understand whether play is enjoyable, we must ask: How do we define *enjoyable*? Each of us can certainly distinguish between experiences that are enjoyable and those that are not—that is, we know an enjoyable experience when we experience one! Indeed, we may even know when an experience has been enjoyable for others, including nonhuman animals, based on gestures, expressions, or behaviors normally associated with pleasurable events (e.g., smiling, laughing, closing eyes when touched, tail wagging). Can we, however, come up with a definition that pinpoints what it means for something to be enjoyable across a wide range of taxa? Probably not. What constitutes an enjoyable experience for humans may not qualify as enjoyable for nonhuman taxa. Furthermore, there might be substantial variation *within taxa* in what types of activities are deemed enjoyable. Within our own species, hiking and camping may be a way of life for some people (hence, we assume that it is enjoyable), while others may avoid such activities like the plague. Propelling oneself from an airplane may be an enjoyable experience for some individuals but an absolutely miserable experience for others. This extended discourse simply demonstrates how difficult it might be to label play as enjoyable.

Nevertheless, let's go out on a limb to construct an argument that it is, in principle, possible to know whether play is enjoyable.

Imagine that we conduct a large-scale study on neurobiological correlates of play in humans. To do this, we survey thousands of human subjects to determine what types of play each *individual* considers to be enjoyable. We then allow these subjects to engage in their activity of choice while connected to a contraption that records brain activity. Astoundingly, we find that the same region of the brain "lights up" irrespective of the type of play undertaken by our human subjects (recall that these activities were all considered enjoyable in the survey). These results suggest that a specific brain region responds to performing "enjoyable" activities. If it turns out that other vertebrate taxa have brain regions that are homologous (similar in developmental origin) to the area that expressed the most activity in humans, we could conduct an interesting comparative analysis. The first step would be to document instances of play in a wide variety of animals. Next, we could catalogue the brain activity of these animals while they play. Does play in nonhuman animals lead to similar brain activity patterns as we observed in humans? If so, we would have speculative evidence (at best) that play *might* be enjoyable for nonhuman taxa. If not, is it possible that in nonhuman animals different brain regions respond to enjoyable experiences? Are there drastic differences in the "pleasure centers" of the brain among taxa? Is it possible that animals simply do not enjoy play? These types of questions are difficult to answer, especially because we simply have no way of asking an animal whether it enjoyed interacting with the toy that was placed in its cage, whether it found pleasure in engaging in locomotor activities, or whether it had a good time tumbling around with its brother. Nevertheless, the fact that we may never *know* whether play is actually enjoyable for nonhuman animals does not preclude our hypothesizing about such an intriguing concept!

3. Gordon Burghardt has described object play in a turtle in the Washington Zoo. The turtle, named Pigface, played with new objects thrown in its pool. Before objects were introduced into its environment, Pigface was in the habit of clawing on his own limbs and neck, causing infection and fungal growth. Once the play objects were introduced, however, this self-destructive behavior dissipated to a great extent. Why do you think that might be? How could this sort of study help in the design of animal habitats in zoos?

It is not uncommon for animals in captivity to exhibit stereotyped behavior, defined by Marriner and Drickamer (1994) as the "uniform repetition of a motor pattern that occurs at a higher frequency than considered typical for a species when observed in a natural environment." Self-injurious behavior could be considered a specific form of stereotypy involving the overexpression of behaviors such as grooming, aggression, and so forth. Indeed, stereotyped self-injurious behavior constitutes a growing problem for captive animals (Tiefenbacher et al., 2000; Novak, 2003). A variety of stereotyped behaviors have been linked to restricted or adverse captive conditions, and it appears as if various forms of environmental enrichment successfully suppress abnormal behavior (e.g., increasing habitat complexity, adding novel objects; Powell et al., 1999, 2000; Burghardt et al., 1996). In the case of Pigface, it may very well have been that stereotyped self-injurious behavior arose because his captive environment provided inadequate stimulation. The introduction of new objects (e.g., basketballs, sticks, hoses) into Pigface's pool could have enhanced the novelty of his environment, thereby reducing self-destructive behavior (Burghardt et al., 1996; Krause et al., 1999). Alternatively, the objects thrown into Pigface's pool could have served as an outlet for abnormal aggressive tendencies (possibly spawned by the captive conditions)—that is, Pigface could now manipulate the object rather than hurting himself. Burghardt's research on soft-shelled turtles links the concepts of environmental enrichment, play, and animal welfare and provides some interesting clues to preserving "normal" animal behavior in captive settings. A review by Mellen and MacPhee (2001) also stresses the careful implementation of environmental enrichment programs to increase the welfare of zoo and aquarium animals. Recognizing the importance of environmental enrichment may stimulate the design of more appropriate settings for captive animals. Furthermore, such programs might increase the efficacy of captive breeding programs and promote the exhibition of natural behaviors in zoo, aquarium, and laboratory animals.

4. Think about play in young children. Does reading a book for pleasure count as play? Does watching a movie or television or playing a video game count as play? If they are considered play, how might these activities fit into Spinka's hypotheses about play?

According to the definition proposed by Bekoff and Byers (see "Defining Play" and Discussion Question 1 above), we could argue that both reading books and playing video games should be considered play. After all, each involves motor activity, is performed postnatally, appears (at least to the general onlooker) to be purposeless, and involves motor patterns usually associated with other contexts. Now let us consider the functional "training for the unexpected" definition proposed by Spinka et al. (2001): "Play functions to increase the versatility of movements used to recover from sudden shocks such as loss of balance and falling over, and to enhance the ability to cope emotionally with unexpected stressful situations." How does this definition apply to playing video games and reading books? Anyone who is marginally familiar with today's brand of video games will notice a few things: (1) success requires exceptional hand-eye coordination, (2) unexpected events are commonplace, and (3) repeated equilibrium-compromising episodes such as falling, crashing, flipping, and diving seem to occur with gut-wrenching frequency. Playing video games may thus be a form of play that prepares a young child for the roller coaster ride that we call life! More specifically, playing video games may increase the *versatility of movements* by fine-tuning hand-eye coordination skills and depth perception. Because modern-day computer programmers implement scenarios ripe with unexpected, stressful virtual events, it is likely that playing video games also trains young children in crisis management—that is, the ability to cope emotionally with wins, losses, and ties in the game of life.

Similar arguments can be made for reading books. Although it is unlikely that a young child will pick up novels that could double as doorstops, many of the books they read still use unexpected plot twists, drama, romance, mystery, or sheer horror to draw the reader's undivided attention. In this sense, reading books might allow young children to "rehearse the emotional aspects of being surprised" (Spinka et al., 2001, p. 144). Based on these descriptions, it should be relatively clear that reading books and playing video games adhere to at least two of the predictions provided in this chapter: (1) the amount of play experienced will affect an animal's ability to handle unexpected events, and (2) play should have measurable effects on an animal's somatosensory, motor, and emotion centers.

5. Some researchers have suggested that play facilitates "creativity." After constructing your own definition of creativity, how would you test this hypothesis? Can you construct tests that both measure behavior and neurobiological/endocrinological correlates of play?

Let's define creativity as the quality of being able to make or bring into existence something new. The generality of this definition is appealing and particularly useful for answering questions about creativity in nonhuman animals because it requires only that an animal display the ability to be innovative. Chapter 5 of this textbook shows that nonhuman animals are capable of bringing into existence something new. Potato and wheat washing in Japanese macaques and modification of tools for specific purposes in New Caledonian crows are just two examples of the innovative capacities of nonhuman animals (see references in Chapter 5 text and this manual).

How could we test whether play facilitates creativity (in our case, innovative behavior)? Intuitively, we would need treatments in which our subjects are either allowed to play or are prevented from playing. With respect to social play, this would entail housing some subjects in groups and other subjects in isolation (or at least in enclosures that provided visual but not physical contact with others). Isolation or the lack of physical contact with others could affect an animal's propensity to innovate irrespective of the opportunity to play (e.g., if isolation stifles innovative behavior for reasons other than the absence of social playmates). Thus, we might want to steer clear of social play for the time being. Locomotor play also poses some difficulties in terms of designing controlled experiments. How do we prevent an animal from skipping, jumping, or tumbling without introducing some confounding factors? Binding our subjects could limit both play and innovative behavior if, for instance, appendages are necessary for the innovative product to be realized. For these reasons, let us focus on **object play** because controlling an animal's access to "toys" can be achieved in a relatively straightforward manner.

In our experiment, we will house the subjects individually in seminatural enclosures. Half of our subjects will have access to objects, while the other half will not. An army of observers will then document all of the behaviors exhibited by the test animals over the course of the study, including the frequency of interaction with the object and any instances of innovation. If play facilitates creativity, we might expect individuals that were exposed to (and played with) objects to demonstrate a greater capacity to innovate. Furthermore, we might expect a strong correlation between the frequency of play (in the object present condition) and the frequency of innovation.

Assessing the neurobiological/endocrinological correlates of play could be accomplished in a number of ways, a few of which are highlighted here. First, we could record and compare neuronal activity of animals in the object-present versus object-absent conditions using awake-behaving protocols (Ramcharan et al., 2003). Second, we could obtain blood samples from the animals in the object-present versus object-absent conditions both before and after the trial period. These blood samples could then be used to assay, for instance, androgen, glucocorticoid, gonadotropin, and catecholamine levels and to facilitate comparisons in hormone titers among animals in each experimental group. Third, we could evaluate whether play elicits changes in brain neuropeptide production (e.g., corticotropin-releasing factor), receptor densities, neuronal growth, or neuronal morphology using a variety of neuromolecular techniques.

MULTIPLE-CHOICE QUESTIONS

1. Cerebellar synaptogenesis is likely to be one benefit of
   a. object play.
   b. locomotor play.
   c. social play.
   d. locomotor and social play.
   e. object and locomotor play.

2. Which of the following statements does *not* relate to "self-handicapping" behavior in animals?
   a. Self-handicapping provides young animals with the opportunity to recognize that they are involved in play.
   b. Older individuals allow younger subordinates to assume the dominant role during play.
   c. Self-handicapping is a means by which young individuals gain benefits by cheating during play.
   d. Older individuals perform some act at a level well below what they are capable of when playing with younger individuals.
   e. Self-handicapping occurs during social play.

3. Siviy's work on play fighting in rats suggests that
   a. play behavior is controlled by one small region of the brain.
   b. play behavior is not influenced by brain neurochemistry.
   c. neural activity in the parafascicular area of the brain is not related to play fighting.
   d. dopamine inhibits play behavior in animals.
   e. play may serve as a mechanism for coping with stress throughout development.

4. Greater endurance, increased strength, and increased motor skills have all been proposed as potential benefits of
   a. social play.
   b. locomotor play.
   c. self-handicapping play.
   d. object play.
   e. all forms of play.

5. Which of the following statements regarding object play is *false?*
   a. Juveniles are predicted to engage in more object play than adults.
   b. The frequency of object play in cheetah cubs corresponds with the cubs' prey handling efficiency.
   c. Object play provides many benefits with no associated costs.
   d. Adults in species with complex behavioral repertoires may master difficult skills through object play.
   e. The types of objects that raven juveniles manipulate influence their reaction to encountering similar items during adulthood.

6. Spinka and his colleagues proposed that play behavior
   a. should have measurable effects on somatosensory, motor, and emotion centers.
   b. can only be exhibited in animals that live in social groups.
   c. allows animals to develop the physical and psychological skills to handle unexpected events in which they experience a loss of control.
   d. will not change over the lifetime of an individual, particularly if the frequency of unexpected events changes at a rapid rate.
   e. a and c

7. Which of the following statements applies to Pellis and Iwaniuk's study of play in muriod rodents?
   a. Species-specific play fighting complexity scores mapped well onto the muriod rodent phylogeny.
   b. Ancestral muriod rodents likely engaged in very simple forms of play.
   c. Play behavior can only become less complex over evolutionary time.
   d. Male-female association patterns did not correlate well with play complexity.

    e. Play fighting repertoires could not have evolved independently in differ-
ent species of muriod rodents over time.

8. Which of the following functions have been proposed for social play?
    a. aids in the development of cognitive skills
    b. assists in establishing long-lasting social bonds
    c. provides physical skills that could be useful later in life
    d. a and c
    e. all of the above

9. In Belding's ground squirrels, males engage in
    a. more sexual play than females, but the same level of play fighting as
       females.
    b. more sexual play and more play fighting than females.
    c. less sexual play and more play fighting than females.
    d. the same level of both sexual play and play fighting as females.
    e. the same level of sexual play as females but less play fighting than
       females.

10. Neurobiological studies of c-fos expression have linked play behavior with
    a. a precise neural circuit.
    b. neurogenesis.
    c. the stress response.
    d. social learning and cultural transmission.
    e. creativity and learning.

REVIEW AND CHALLENGE QUESTIONS

1. Compare and contrast the benefits and costs associated with object, locomotor, and social play. Can you think of any additional benefits and costs of
play that were not discussed in this chapter? If so, describe how these benefits
and costs might influence play behavior.

2. In the last section of this chapter, you were introduced to phylogenetic
analyses of play. Pellis and Iwaniuk's (1999) analyses spurred some interesting
discussion about the evolution of simple versus complex play. What selective
forces might favor simple play? What selective forces might favor complex play?

3. Devise at least two proximate explanations for why the frequency of play behavior might increase in groups of animals that are provided with supplemental
food resources.

4. Describe Bekoff's (2000) three postulates regarding how young animals distinguish play from nonplay. How do Bekoff's postulates draw on ideas related to
both individual and social learning?

5. How would you go about testing the long-term fitness benefits of play? Why are longitudinal empirical or observational studies important for examining the evolutionary ramifications of play?

ANSWER KEY FOR MULTIPLE-CHOICE QUESTIONS

1.	d	6.	e
2.	c	7.	d
3.	e	8.	e
4.	b	9.	a
5.	c	10.	e

CHAPTER 16 | Aging and Disease

DISCUSSION QUESTIONS

1. What is the difference between aging and senescence? Given the definition in the chapter, is it possible that animals might not only fail to senesce, but they might actually have survival probabilities that are the exact opposite of those associated with senescence? What would a chart of survival probabilities look like? Do you think this is likely in nature? Why or why not?

Aging refers to the process by which organisms get older. Between today and tomorrow, you will have aged one day; between this year and next, you will have aged one year. In contrast, **senescence** refers to age-specific mortality and particularly to an increased probability of dying (or decreased probability of survival) with age. When we ask whether it is possible for animals *not* to senesce, we are not proposing that animals do not age but rather that the probability of survival does not change with age. Similarly, when we ask whether animals may have survival probabilities that are the exact opposite of those associated with senescence, we must consider whether there are some instances where the probability of dying *decreases* with age. Population ecology is best suited to answer such questions because an entire theory—life history and survivorship—has been dedicated to examining the patterns of mortality with age in a diverse array of organisms, plants and animals alike (Begon et al., 1996). Indeed, ecologists have identified three survivorship curves—that is, the number of individuals in a given population that survive to the next age class (see Figure 4.12 in Begon et al., 1996):

Type I. The probability of dying increases with age (senescence as defined in the chapter).

Type II. The probability of dying remains constant throughout the lifetime of the organism.

Type III. The probability of dying decreases with age (the polar opposite of senescence).

Organisms that follow a Type II survivorship curve would, based on our definition of senescence, fail to senesce. In fact, for organisms that experience age-independent risks of predation or parasitism, the probability of dying might be the same throughout life. Alternatively, if different (but equally effective) mortality risks exist at different stages of life, one might expect the probability of dying to remain constant across all age classes. Organisms that exhibit Type III survivorship curves would show the exact opposite pattern of mortality than is usually associated with senescence—that is, the risk of dying would be greatest when young and least when old. Imagine a fish species in which tens of thousands of eggs are fertilized but only a few survive to adulthood due to substantial predation pressures on the larvae. Because age is tightly linked with size in fish—that is, indeterminate growth—older fish will be larger and thus may not be subject to such predation pressures. Once a critical age (size) is reached, the probability of dying decreases.

It is important to recognize that all organisms do not fit nicely within this three-layered survivorship scheme. In fact, patterns of mortality likely fall along a continuum from Type I to Type III. Nonetheless, the fact that some organisms *do* conform to one of the three survivorship curves suggests that patterns of dying where senescence is absent and patterns that oppose senescence are common in nature (Strassman et al., 1997; Tanner, 2001).

2. What might be an adaptationist's most basic argument against the antagonistic pleiotropy hypothesis? Hint: This hypothesis assumes that pleiotropic effects cannot be broken down.

Antagonistic pleiotropy refers to a situation in which one gene has multiple effects at different periods during an organism's lifetime. Specifically, this gene may have a positive effect (e.g., increased fecundity) early in life and a negative effect (e.g., reduced life span) later in life. According to Williams's (1957) hypothesis, positive effects that are manifest early in life, when there is still ample reproductive opportunity, should be selected for and can potentially override the antagonistic effects that occur as the organism ages. If the positive and negative effects of a particular gene cannot be broken down— that is, selection cannot favor the positive trait without also favoring the negative trait—then, with respect to strict adaptationism, we have a conundrum on our hands. How can selection operate so as to favor traits that compromise fitness even if some aspect of the underlying genetics enhances fitness early on in life? On the one hand, we might expect these genetically correlated, antagonistic traits to be selected against for the simple reason that there are negative consequences associated with the trait (or gene) in question. But if the benefits associated with early expression of the gene outweigh the costs that accrue later in life, then selection may favor the gene despite its antagonistic effects. On the other hand, natural selection may act to break down pleiotropic effects, such that the negative effects of the gene in question are eliminated while still maintaining the positive effects.

We have come up with three tentative options for antagonistic pleiotropy: (1) natural selection favors the positive effects over the negative effects, and thus antagonistic pleiotropy persists, (2) natural selection eliminates both traits as a consequence of the detrimental age-related effects, or (3) natural selection breaks down the pleiotropic relationship, selects for the positive effects, and selects against the negative effects. With respect to the first two options, which still assume that pleiotropic effects cannot be dissected, the fate of the pleiotropic interaction likely rests with the *relative* fitness consequences of the antagonism—that is, selection "weighs" the benefits and costs associated with age-related gene expression patterns. Here, as the benefits of maintaining the pleiotropic interaction increase relative to the costs, the more likely selection might be to maintain genes that have age-related "Jekyll and Hyde" expression patterns. The third option recognizes that natural selection may indeed be powerful enough to sever the pleiotropic interaction, thereby paving the way for independent selection on the two traits within a population. (For recent articles on this and related topics associated with antagonistic pleiotropy—for example, the maintenance of stable polymorphisms—refer to a pair of papers by Phelan et al., 2003, and Archer et al., 2003, on fruit flies, as well as papers by Curtsinger et al., 1994, Hedrick, 1999, and Kruuk et al., 2002.)

3. If glucocorticoids are linked to disease, senescence, and aging, why hasn't natural selection significantly reduced levels of these hormones?

In the "Glucocorticoids and Aging" section of this chapter, you became familiar with some of the adverse effects of prolonged **glucocorticoid** secretion, including degeneration of the hippocampus and associated learning capabilities, inhibition of nerve growth, and so on. Given that prolonged exposure to high levels of glucocorticoids can have devastating effects, why hasn't natural selection reduced levels of these hormones? Recall from Chapter 3 that, in the short term, glucocorticoids are essential for shaping an organism's behavioral responses (e.g., movement) and metabolic responses (e.g., increased production and mobilization of energy sources) to stressful events. In this sense, glucocorticoid secretion enhances the probability of survival in the face of environmental stressors. If the survival benefits of glucocorticoid secretion trump the long-term costs, then natural selection should favor the release of such hormones when environmental challenges present themselves. But this is not to say that natural selection would favor animals that constantly release glucocorticoids. Rather, mechanisms that allow an animal to escape the environmental perturbation and thus avoid perpetually high levels of glucocorticoids should be selectively advantageous. A recent article by McEwen and Wingfield (2003) clearly articulates the pros and cons of glucocorticoid secretion and the relationships that exist between an organism's life history, environmental conditions, energy balance, and stress hormone levels.

4. If animals, particularly primates, use self-medication, what impact might this have on the relationship between conservation biology and the medical sciences?

When animals eat materials that have virtually no nutritive value (e.g., plant secondary compounds, dirt), one is compelled to ask: Why would such materials be incorporated into the diet? In several fascinating accounts (some of which do not entail the ingestion of materials), this chapter provides a tentative reason why animals might do this: self-medication. The prevention and treatment of diseases is of great concern to human and nonhuman animals alike, particularly because such behavior may reduce the fitness costs associated with bacterial, viral, or parasitic infections. Approximately half of today's current pharmaceuticals are derived from natural plant products (Cowan, 1999), and recent pharmaceutical research has recognized the vast importance that natural chemicals have had, and continue to have, in the development of new preventative or therapeutic drugs (McChesney, 1993; Clark, 1996; DeSmet, 1997; Pandy, 1998). This sets the stage for an interesting collaboration between ethologists, conservation biologists, and pharmaceutical researchers. By observing the behavior of animals, ethologists may pinpoint naturally derived products that have antimicrobial, antiviral, or antiparasitic properties—that is, they observe whether animals that consume such products are less susceptible to disease than animals that do not consume the products. Given our relatively recent common ancestry with other primates (e.g., chimpanzees, bonobos), we might predict that naturally derived medicines used by these primates would be especially effective at combating disease in humans. Drawing from the keen observations of ethologists, pharmaceutical and medical researchers could then test the medicinal value of the natural products utilized by primate populations (e.g., by taking samples of certain plants from the field and conducting rigorous medical research on putative antidisease chemicals contained within the plant). Clearly, cross talk between ethologists and medical scientists would facilitate identification of preventative or therapeutic drugs, thereby quickening the pace of medical discovery. But there is a twist to this story. Without implementing proper conservation efforts that aim to either maintain or restore primate habitats, the future of such ethological-medical cross talk may be bleak. Ethology facilitated drug discovery may serve as an incentive to conserve our dwindling habitats and the organisms that occupy these habitats. After all, if we cannot observe the self-medication behavior of animals, particularly primates, it might be exponentially more difficult to identify plants with medicinal properties—that is, the primates would no longer be identifying these plants for us. Similarly, if primate habitats are neglected, we may also lose the opportunity of pinpointing key natural pharmaceutical products.

5. *Imagine you are working with some species of fish in which individuals form associations with other group members when foraging, avoiding predators, and so on. How might you go about constructing laboratory experiments to examine how important avoiding diseased conspecifics is when compared to other factors in choosing associates?*

In some species, associating with conspecifics bears many fruits in terms of increased foraging success, vigilance, information gathering, and so on. But associating with the *wrong* individuals may be costly. For instance, if an animal associates with a diseased conspecific, then its likelihood of contracting the disease increases (and its fitness may be compromised). Thus, it might be beneficial for an animal to have the means by which to distinguish diseased from healthy individuals so that it can draw on such information when choosing associates. For our purposes, let's revisit one of the experiments described in the "Learning and Antipredator Behavior" section of Chapter 11. Alfieri (2000) demonstrated that guppies (*Poecilia reticulata*) prefer to associate with individuals that are predator-experienced. Although the proximate mechanisms underlying this choice remain mysterious, we can simply assume that guppies have some way of distinguishing between predator-experienced and predator-inexperienced individuals (refer to your answer to Review Question 3 in Chapter 11). Now we are primed to ask the question of how disease and predator experience interact when guppies choose associates. To address this question empirically, we could establish a number of preference trials using a "focal" guppy (the one choosing) and two potential partners. The focal guppy would be positioned in the center of an aquarium and the two partners at opposite ends of the apparatus. Some of the potential partners would be exposed to bacterial infection (the diseased treatment) several days before the preference trials begin while other potential partners would not be exposed to bacterial infection (the healthy treatment). In addition, some individuals in each of the diseased and healthy treatments would be exposed to a predator (predator-experienced, PE), while others would remain naive to predators (predator-inexperienced, PI). We would allow the focal guppy to choose between the following pairs of associates: (a) PE healthy vs. PI healthy, (b) PI diseased vs. PI healthy, (c) PE diseased vs. PE healthy, (d) PE diseased vs. PI healthy, (e) PE healthy vs. PI diseased, (f) PE diseased vs. PI diseased.

Treatments (a) and (f) allow you to test whether the guppies prefer predator-experienced over predator-inexperienced individuals when both partners are in the same condition (as in Alfieri, 2000). Treatments (b) and (c) allow you to test whether guppies prefer healthy over diseased animals when both partners have similar experience with predators. Treatments (d) and (e) facilitate an examination of the relative importance of disease and predator experience in choosing associates. For the sake of argument, let's assume that our focal guppies demonstrate a preference for experienced partners—that is, they choose to associate with experienced partners *significantly more* than inexperienced partners in both treatment (a) and treatment (f). Let us also assume that, in treatments (b) and (c), our focal guppies prefer healthy over diseased conspecifics when all else is equal. Now suppose you find that the focal guppies choose predator-experienced partners *significantly more* in treatment (a) than they did in treatment (d). This would suggest that guppies are capable of detecting the health of potential partners and that information available about a partner's condition overrides information about a partner's experience with predators. Another piece of evidence to support this claim would be if the focal guppies showed an even greater aversion to inexperienced partners in treatment (e) than in treatment (a). There are sure to be many alternative ways of testing hypotheses about the relative roles of disease and predator experience in shaping associative preference. But the experiments described above provide a template for examining the interactions between multiple factors (in this case, disease and predator experience) in sculpting animal associations.

MULTIPLE-CHOICE QUESTIONS

1. George Williams's version of antagonistic pleiotropy refers to a phenomenon by which
   a. a single gene has more than one effect on an organism.
   b. two genes, each of which has a negative effect when expressed alone, have substantial positive effects when expressed together.
   c. one gene can have increasingly negative effects on fitness as an organism ages.
   d. two separate genes, coding for the same trait, have opposite effects on fitness.
   e. one gene can have a positive effect on fitness at time 1 but a negative effect on fitness at time 2.

2. Senescence occurs when the probability of dying
   a. is lowest in older individuals.
   b. increases with increasing age.
   c. remains constant across all age classes.
   d. increases up to a certain age and then decreases dramatically.
   e. is highest in middle-aged animals.

3. Which of the following effects is *not* associated with prolonged exposure to glucocorticoids?
   a. decreased hippocampal deterioration
   b. onset of pathologies such as diabetes and hypertension
   c. failed neuron repair
   d. compromised immune system
   e. inhibition of nerve growth

4. Patterns of spice use across the world are correlated with the
   a. types of spices located in any given region.
   b. recently discovered anti-aging properties of particular spices.
   c. ability of spices to induce perspiration.
   d. mean annual temperature and probability of food spoilage.
   e. nutritional value of the spice.

5. Which of the following statements is *not* related to the disposable soma theory?
   a. Decreased longevity results from diverting resources away from bodily maintenance and repair.
   b. Species that invest little in traits related to reproduction will live longer than species that invest a great deal in reproductive traits.
   c. Animals don't need to invest energy in maintenance and repair until negative pleiotropic effects begin to occur.
   d. Longevity will be lower in the sex that invests more in reproduction.
   e. A finite amount of energy is available to an organism at any given time.

6. Heat-shock proteins (hsp) function as molecular chaperones that
   a. transport glucocorticoids to the brain.
   b. are expressed more often in old animals than in young animals.
   c. trigger perspiration and other types of "cooling" processes when body temperature exceeds some threshold.
   d. bind to proteins that have been damaged by heat stress, assist in their disposal, and prevent buildup of toxic molecules in the cell.
   e. expedite the aging process by destroying healthy cells and depositing these cells in the brain.

7. Which of the following behaviors represents a potential form of preventative self-medication?
   a. depositing antibacterial plant substances in one's nest
   b. rubbing fruits, leaves, or vines against one's fur
   c. consuming soil, dirt, or rocks
   d. spreading crushed ants onto one's plumage
   e. all of the above

8. Of the factors listed below, which one has gained empirical support in terms of its longevity-enhancing effects?
   a. increased age at first reproduction in females
   b. increased courtship vigor in males
   c. decreased use of self-medication in both sexes
   d. increased investment in large body size in males
   e. decreased investment in maintenance and repair in both sexes

9. Antagonistic pleiotropy has been linked to senescence in which of the following ways?
   a. When the negative effects of a pleiotropic gene are "turned on," the animal experiences an immediate and dramatic decrease in survival probability.
   b. Senescence represents the accumulation of the negative effects of pleiotropic genes in aging animals.
   c. As the positive effects of a pleiotropic gene increase, so too does the rate at which the animal senesces.
   d. The positive and negative effects of a pleiotropic gene are directly proportional to one another and to the rate of senescence.
   e. Senescence and antagonistic pleiotropy are unrelated concepts.

10. Which of the following statements concerning disease and disease avoidance in gray tree frogs (*Hyla versicolor*) is *not* correct?
    a. The snail *Pseudosuccinea columella* is an intermediate host for a trematode parasite that infects larval frogs.
    b. Choice of oviposition sites affects larval performance and mortality.
    c. *H. versicolor* adults alter oviposition decisions based on the presence or absence of snails.
    d. *H. versicolor* adults do not change oviposition decisions based on the density of snails.
    e. Trematode infection can lead to a reduction in frog survival and growth rates.

Review and Challenge Questions

1. Describe the disposable soma theory and how it relates to the notion of tradeoffs. Also discuss some of the predictions of the disposable soma theory as they relate to differences in senescence across species or sexes.

2. In this chapter, you were introduced to two nonmutually exclusive theories of senescence—antagonistic pleiotropy and the disposable soma theory. Conduct a small-scale review of the enormous literature on senescence and describe at least one additional theory that poses an explanation for why animals senesce.

3. Outline the importance of heat-shock proteins (hsp) in the process of senescence. Construct an ultimate (rather than proximate) argument about why heat-shock proteins may have evolved. Also, why do you think the universality and relatively conserved nature of heat-shock proteins across taxa stimulated a fair bit of attention with respect to studies on senescence?

4. Natural selection might favor animals that are capable of identifying and avoiding areas (or conspecifics) that are infested with parasites. In Chapter 13,

you were introduced to the ideal free distribution model. How might a habitat's parasite load or the parasite load of individuals occupying a particular habitat change the predictions of the ideal free distribution model? To answer this question, imagine two habitats—one that is rich in both resources and parasites and one that has poor resource quality but few parasites. How might the ideal free distribution equilibrium change?

5. You are now familiar with Kiesecker and colleagues' (1999) study on how tadpoles avoid diseased conspecifics. Their study indicated that tadpoles use chemical cues to distinguish infected from noninfected individuals. Design an experiment that could tease apart the importance of visual and chemical cues in tadpole disease avoidance behavior. What types of chemical cues might be used by these tadpoles? Do you think chemical cues would be as important in terrestrial habitats (rather than the aquatic habitats in which tadpoles live)?

ANSWER KEY FOR MULTIPLE-CHOICE QUESTIONS

1.	e	6.	d
2.	b	7.	e
3.	a	8.	a
4.	d	9.	b
5.	c	10.	d

CHAPTER 17

Animal Personalities

DISCUSSION QUESTIONS

1. Go to the monkey exhibit at your local zoo and pick four individual monkeys to observe for at least four hours. Record all the information you can on each individual ("grooms," "eats," "attacks," "retreats," "sleeps," "plays," and so on), and if possible, note the proximity of the animals you are studying to others in the group. From your observations, can you suggest a list of behaviors that you might focus on during a longer, more controlled, study of personality in the population that you are observing?

A common theme throughout this chapter is the importance of behavioral consistency in assigning personality traits. During four hours of intense observation of monkeys at the local zoo, you may be awestruck by the vast behavioral repertoires that these animals exhibit—grooming, eating, mating, courting, playing, and so on. Using your keen ethological eye, you also may notice some regularity in individual behavior amidst incredible between-individual variation. Some monkeys consistently eat while hanging upside down, while others seem to prefer having both feet firmly on the ground (or on a branch) while indulging. Some female monkeys appear to groom their young more frequently than others, despite the fact that (as you learned from the monkey caretaker) little variation in parasite loads or "dirtiness" exists among the young monkeys. Some individuals appear to use vocalizations as their primary means of communication, while others prefer tactile methods.

After displaying unprecedented enthusiasm for the prospect of studying personality types in this group of monkeys, the zoo names you as their primary behavioral specialist. You propose to conduct a five-year observational study with the aim of unveiling significant behavioral consistencies in this monkey population. Because the zoo is interested in captive breeding programs for these monkeys and in limiting within-group hostility, you choose to focus on two general categories of behavior: (1) mating and parental care, and (2) unpleasant behavior. Within each of these general categories, you record many types of related behavior. For instance, in the "mating and parental care" category, you document offspring grooming, protective behavior, putative instances of teaching, willingness to mate when in estrous, and so on. In the "unpleasant behavior" category, you document each individual's propensity to start fights, instances of apparently unwarranted violence, refusal to share or reciprocate, and so on. You discover remarkable consistency within each behavioral category (as was predicted from your initial observations) and, as a result, are able to provide management suggestions to the zoo concerning individuals who might best be suited for captive breeding programs or who have a penchant for disrupting group harmony (and thus might be a catalyst for increasing group-wide stress levels). As described in Discussion Question 3 of Chapter 15, it may also be useful to assess individual consistency in abnormal behaviors such as self-mutilation or abnormal stereotypes so as to identify "at risk" individuals or initiate studies that can pinpoint potential causes of distress. Lastly, you may opt to conduct cross-population comparisons (possibly in collaboration with another zoo) to assess whether monkey groups as a whole adopt certain personality traits (e.g., via culturally transmitted information) that differ from those adopted by groups in other localities.

2. How would you construct an experiment to examine whether boldness and/or behavioral inhibition are heritable traits?

In Chapter 2, you were introduced to two techniques often employed to assess narrow-sense heritability—truncation selection and **parent-offspring regression**. Because we already touched upon truncation selection experiments in detail (see Chapter 5, Discussion Question 5), we will assess the heritability of boldness and/or behavioral inhibition using parent-offspring regression here. First, let us take a brief hiatus from the question at hand and revisit the logic underlying the parent-offspring regression method.

If the trait in question has a genetic component and if parents pass genes on to their offspring, then we would expect offspring to exhibit traits similar to those of their parents. When a large population of the parental generation is assayed, we may find a considerable amount of variation in the focal trait and we would predict variation in the subsequent offspring to map onto parental variation. To understand the relationship between trait variation in the parental and offspring generations, we conduct a regression analysis. If the resulting correlation between trait variation in the parent and offspring generations is *significantly* positive, we can be relatively confident that narrow-sense heritability is high—that is, that the trait has a substantial heritable component.

Given this background information, we are now poised to address whether boldness or behavioral inhibition are heritable. To make our experimental efforts a bit less time intensive, let us select a species with relatively short generation times—say, crickets. Furthermore, to reduce the amount of environmental variance that could contribute to trait variation, we select a population that inhabits a relatively stable environment. While observing our population of crickets, we notice that some individuals have a greater propensity to start fights than others and that individuals display remarkable consistency in this trait throughout their lifetime, regardless of past fighting experience. Let us also assume that only the males of this species engage in aggressive interactions. Males that consistently instigate aggressive interactions considered to be *bold*, while males that refrain from instigating fights are considered to be *inhibited*.

Prior to the mating season, we partition our population of crickets (composed of thousands of similarly sized individuals) into a focal group (n = 200) and an opponent group (n = 2000). We then expose each of our male focal crickets to ten novel opponents over the course of one month and document all fighting incidents and the identity of the instigator, never exposing any of the males to the same opponent and never using any of the opponents twice. Following these trials, we calculate the proportion of contests in which the focal cricket initiates the encounter (e.g., approaches its opponent or instigates antennal probing), and we determine the population distribution for this behavioral trait. Next, we allow the males to mate with virgin females of the same population, transfer the females to an oviposition site, and rear the offspring. We then subject all male offspring to the same fighting trials described above *at the same age* that their fathers were tested to control for any age-related effects. We record the proportion of fights instigated by each offspring and construct an offspring distribution. The question then is whether the distribution of offspring boldness (fight initiation) maps well onto the distribution of parent (father) boldness. When conducting the regression analysis, we find a significant positive correlation between fight instigation probabilities in the parental and offspring generations, suggesting that boldness is indeed heritable in our cricket population.

Parent-offspring regression analyses are often not as straightforward as the study above purports. Thus, you are encouraged to conduct some independent research on, for instance, different types of parent-offspring regression analyses (e.g., one-parent offspring regression, in which the traits of either the mother *or* father are considered; mid-parent-offspring regression, in which the traits of both parents are considered), maternal effects, and so forth (see Gibert et al., 1998; Hoffmann, 1999; Keller et al., 2001, for recent treatments).

3. Besides the ones mentioned in this chapter, what general costs and benefits might you associate with being bold or inhibited? Next pick a particular species you are familiar with and create a list of the potential costs and benefits of boldness and shyness in that species.

In the "Guppies, Boldness, and Predator Inspection" section of this chapter, you were introduced to some of the costs and benefits that bold, inspector guppies might experience. In terms of benefits, bold guppies were both more attractive to females and were able to obtain more information about potential predators (e.g., where the predator is lurking, whether the predator is hungry, how close the predator is to one's group). But bold guppies were also more prone to be eaten by voracious predators—quite the cost! Our primary mission is to think about some additional costs and benefits associated with being bold or behaviorally inhibited. Any list of added costs and benefits will necessarily be incomplete, but we will try to touch on some of interesting ones here.

a. Benefits of Boldness
(1) *Increased access to resources (or prime feeding spots).* If bold individuals engage in more exploratory behavior than inhibited animals, as the predator inspection experiments seem to indicate, then they may have an increased probability of stumbling upon new, lucrative foraging sites, water holes, and so on.
(2) *Fortified stress response.* If bold individuals encounter stressful situations more often, they may develop more efficient physiological or behavioral coping strategies than inhibited individuals (but see below for costs).
(3) *Scramble competition advantage.* This benefit relates to (1) in the sense that, if bold individuals encounter prime feeding spots, mates, or any other resource *first*, they can reap the benefits, leaving the "scraps" for their behaviorally inhibited (less exploratory) groupmates.

b. Costs of Boldness
(1) *Energy expenditure.* If bold individuals move about more frequently, they may burn energy at a faster rate; this may be particularly costly when resources are limited.
(2) *Exploratory costs.* Aside from encountering prime feeding sites or mates, exploratory behavior may also increase the probability of meeting dangerous predators or otherwise unpleasant aspects of the environment (e.g., traps, poisonous but not predatory heterospecifics, pathogens, dangerous habitats).
(3) *Physiological costs.* This is simply the flip side of (2) under the "Benefits" heading. Constant exposure to stressful stimuli may have detrimental effects on physiological balance, which may ultimately lead to pathologies, brain degeneration, and aging (see Chapters 3 and 16).

4. Pick up a few recent issues of the journal Animal Behaviour *and scan the titles for anything on "alternative strategies." Once you have found one or two such articles, read them in detail. Is there any mention of personality in these papers? If not, how might you reanalyze the data to see whether the alternative strategies could be construed in light of the work on animal personalities? What other sorts of data could you collect to better understand whether the alternative strategies represent personality types?*

Because conducting literature searches is an integral part of your development as an ethologist, specific articles will not be tackled in this answer. With that being said, however, it is unlikely that the literature you unearth from today's vast databases will address alternative strategies from the perspective of personalities. Why might this be so? First, many studies on alternative strategies document snapshots of individual behavior within a population so as to assess, for instance, differential costs and benefits associated with being a territory holder, sneaker, or satellite. Although these studies are fascinating in their own right, snapshots in time are not conducive to studies on personalities. Rather, longitudinal studies wherein specific individuals are tracked over an extended period of time (or, ideally a lifetime) are necessary to determine behavioral consistency. Second, researchers may be cautious in their terminology, employing the term "alternative strategies" in lieu of "personality," which some might argue is borderline anthropomorphic, to explain between-individual variation and within-individual stasis.

As was clearly shown in the "Bold and Inhibited Pumpkinseeds" section of the chapter, beautifully designed, field-based and laboratory studies on personalities do exist. The question, then, is what sorts of data are critical to figuring out whether alternative strategies qualify as personalities. Most importantly, you would need to design a study that is long enough to document changes (or consistencies) in the behavior of specific individuals over time. As such, you would also need to devise a technique for recognizing animals in your population on an individual basis. Discussion Question 4 in Chapter 13 was also about conducting experiments on alternative strategies. Referring to the answer to that question, you should recognize that the tactics any one individual adopts can be fixed (e.g., when genetically determined) or labile (e.g., when influenced by ecological or social factors). If individuals in your study species exhibit the same strategy throughout their lives, as was the case for lekking male ruffs (see the "Ruff Satellites" section of the text), it might seem fair to consider each of the alternative tactics a different "personality." But if the strategy any one individual employs changes with ecological conditions, social conditions, size, or age, then we would have little evidence to support the existence of stable personality types in our population. Examples of such labile strategies include: (1) territorial if dominant, sneaky if subordinate, (2) sneaky when small, territorial when large, and (3) female when small relative to others in your group, or subordinate but male when relatively large or dominant (Warner et al., 1975; Reavis and Grober, 1998).

5. Besides preventing the death of livestock and selecting guide dogs, can you think of any other practical applications of personality work in animals? How might you construct some experiment to better understand whether the applications you suggest are feasible?

As you learned in the chapter, applied ethological research on animal personalities can have a broad impact on venues ranging from conservation and livestock farming practices to the development of animal-based aid programs for the visually impaired. Are these just isolated incidents where knowledge of animal personalities just happens to be useful? Probably not. To see why, let's first revisit our monkey troop from Discussion Question 1. Despite the "what if" nature of the scenario described in Discussion Question 1, there is some element of truth to the projected applications of studying personalities in zoo animals. For instance, understanding personality traits may facilitate the development of more productive captive breeding programs (e.g., identifying those individuals most likely to breed successfully) and assist in identifying animals that might be a detriment to the integrity of the group. In addition, studying animal personalities may be helpful in deciding which animals are best suited for situations that involve considerable interactions with humans. Clearly, pets that exhibit aggressive tendencies would not be recommended for families with young children. Studies on pet personality traits might help pet stores or animal care centers to discourage young families from adopting pets that would be more likely to be involved in dangerous incidents with humans. This same logic may apply to wildlife and amusement parks, which rely on revenue from "petting zoos" or attendance at animal shows that feature amazing stunts involving both trainers and (potentially deadly) animals. Obviously, accurate assessment of personalities is crucial for these applications to be successful, and this may entail years of research wherein an investigator (1) compiles a suite of relevant behaviors, (2) develops tests to determine the relationship between any given personality and the success rate of a practical application (e.g., fearlessness and passing the guide dog exam), (3) conducts rigorous observation sessions, and (4) determines the reliability of "personality indices" by repeating studies multiple times or by cross-checking his or her data with that of other investigators.

MULTIPLE-CHOICE QUESTIONS

1. Personality differences are defined as
   a. consistent, long-term phenotypic behavioral differences among individuals.
   b. genotypic differences among individuals that, paradoxically, give rise to the same behavior.
   c. short-term genotypic effects on certain behavior patterns.
   d. long-term, but inconsistent manifestations of behavior in a single individual.
   e. phenotypic differences between species.

2. Potential benefits of predator inspection behavior include
   a. identifying whether a predator is a potential danger.
   b. assessing the motivational state of the predator.
   c. announcing to a predator that it has been seen.
   d. obtaining information on how close the predator is to one's group.
   e. all of the above

3. Differences in _____ have been shown between individuals that adopt proactive versus reactive coping styles.
   a. disease susceptibility
   b. noradrenaline levels
   c. immunosuppressive capabilities
   d. aggressive behavior
   e. all of the above

4. Empirical work in guppies (*Poecilia reticulata*) has shown that bold inspectors enjoy which of the following benefits?
   a. decreased mortality risk
   b. feeding priority in a stream
   c. mate attraction
   d. larger energy budget
   e. lower parasite infestation

5. Which of the following statements regarding the work of Lank and his colleagues on ruff leks is *false*?
   a. Male mating strategies are sex-linked traits.
   b. Mating strategies are likely inherited via a single locus with two alleles.
   c. Male mating strategies are not inherited via the sex chromosome.
   d. The allele coding for the satellite strategy is dominant.
   e. none of the above

6. What is the single most important question that a researcher must consider before labeling certain behaviors as personalities?
   a. Do individuals exhibit the same behavior pattern as others in the population?
   b. Do individuals consistently exhibit the same patterns of behavior?
   c. Do individuals within a population differ in their behavioral repertoires?
   d. Do certain individuals behave more economically than others?
   e. Do some individuals invest more energy in one type of behavior than others?

7. Proactive coping styles are associated with
   a. immobility and low aggression levels.
   b. active responses to problems encountered in the environment.
   c. withdrawal from problems encountered in the environment.
   d. territorial control and aggression.
   e. b and d

8. Personality types have been studied most comprehensively by
   a. endocrinologists.
   b. neurobiologists.
   c. ethologists.
   d. psychologists.
   e. geneticists.

9. Which of the following contraptions was used by Wilson and his colleagues to catch "bold" pumpkinseed sunfish?
   a. custom-designed traps
   b. seining nets
   c. bottles
   d. aquarium fish nets
   e. hook and line

10. Gosling's studies on hyenas identified which of the following sets of personality subcategories?
    a. assertiveness, human-directed agreeableness, curiosity, excitability, and sociability
    b. assertiveness, violent tendencies, curiosity, excitability, and sociability
    c. assertiveness, boldness, aggressiveness, excitability, and sociability
    d. assertiveness, boldness, aggressiveness, coping ability, and excitability
    e. behavioral inhibition, boldness, aggressiveness, curiosity, and excitability

REVIEW AND CHALLENGE QUESTIONS

1. Conduct a small-scale search of the animal behavior literature for studies that perform repeatability analyses. Describe the major objective of repeatability analysis and how this technique is relevant to studying animal personalities.

2. Imagine that you have been diligently collecting behavioral data on a particular species of bird for the past ten years. While scanning your data, you discover that: (a) individuals in each population are consistent in the behaviors they exhibit, (b) a fair bit of between-individual behavioral variation exists within a population, and (c) substantial between-population behavioral variation exists. Construct a set of experiments that could tease apart the contribution of genetic versus cultural inheritance in the establishment of putative personality types in your study organism.

3. Discuss the concept of a "coping style" put forth by Koolhaas et al. (1999). How might two drastically different coping styles be equally adaptive? Also, can you think of any ways in which experiences in early life shape the coping style that any given animal adopts?

4. In the interview with Jerome Kagan, you were introduced to the possibility that morphological traits can be altered as a consequence of selection for certain personality traits (e.g., aggression) and vice versa. Artificial selection is widespread in the recreational fisheries industry, and the selection process often modifies both morphological and behavioral traits. Imagine that selection for body size in sport fish also yields consistent differences in aggressive and/or competitive behavior. How might this information be utilized to predict the im-

pact of introducing fisheries-reared sport fish into natural populations of the same species or the viability of the sport fish population?

5. How might we gain a more comprehensive understanding of the mechanisms underlying personality types by integrating ethology and neuroendocrinology?

ANSWER KEY FOR MULTIPLE-CHOICE QUESTIONS

1.	a	6.	b
2.	e	7.	e
3.	e	8.	d
4.	c	9.	a
5.	a	10.	a

LITERATURE CITED

Abrahams, M. V., & Pratt, T. C. (2000). Hormonal manipulation of growth rate and its influence on predator avoidance: Foraging trade-offs. *Canadian Journal of Zoology-Revue Canadienne De Zoologie, 78*, 121–127.

Alfieri, M. (2000). *The interaction effects of experience, learning, and social associations on survival in the guppy, Poecilia reticula*. Ph.D. thesis, University of Louisville, Louisville, KY.

Allen, C., & Bekoff, M. (1995). Biological function, adaptation, and natural design. *Philosophy of Science, 62*, 609–622.

Anderson, C., Cremer, S., & Heinze, J. (2003). Live and let die: Why fighter males of the ant *Cardiocondyla* kill each other but tolerate their winged rivals. *Behavioral Ecology, 14*, 54–62.

Archer, M. A., Phelan, J. P., Beckman, K. A., & Rose, M. R. (2003). Breakdown in correlations during laboratory evolution. II. Selection on stress resistance in *Drosophila* populations. *Evolution, 57*, 536–543.

Arnold, K. E. (2000). Group mobbing behaviour and nest defence in a cooperatively breeding Australian bird. *Ethology, 106*, 385–393.

Arnold, S. J. (1976). Sexual behavior, sexual interference, and sexual defense in the salamanders *Ambystoma maculatum, Ambystoma tigrinum* and *Plethodon jordani*. *Zeitschrift fur Tierpsychologie, 42*, 247–300.

Arthur, W. (2001). Developmental drive: An important determinant of the direction of phenotypic evolution. *Evolution and Development, 3–4*, 271–278.

Austad, S. N., & Fischer, K. E. (1992). Primate longevity—its place in the mammalian scheme. *American Journal of Primatology, 28*, 251–261.

Autumn, K., Ryan, M. J., & Wake, D. B. (2002). Integrating historical and mechanistic biology enhances the study of adaptation. *Quarterly Review of Biology, 77*, 383–408.

Avise, J. C. (2002). *Genetics in the wild*. Washington, DC: Smithsonian Institution Press.

Barlow, G. W. (1998). Sexual-selection models for exaggerated traits are useful but constraining. *American Zoologist, 38,* 59–69.

Bean, D., & Cook, J. M. (2002). Male mating tactics and lethal combat in the non-pollinating fig wasp *Sycoscapter australis*. *Animal Behaviour, 62,* 535–542.

Beauchamp, G. (2003). Group-size effects on vigilance: A search for mechanisms. *Behavioural Processes, 63,* 111–121.

Beauchamp, G., Bélisle, M., & Giraldeau, L.-A. (1997). Influence of conspecific attraction on the spatial distribution of learning foragers in a patchy habitat. *Journal of Animal Ecology, 66,* 671–682.

Bednekoff, P. A. (1997). Mutualism among safe, selfish sentinels: A dynamic game. *American Naturalist, 150,* 373–392.

Begon, M., Harper, J. L., & Townsend, C. R. (1996). *Ecology,* 3rd ed. Oxford: Blackwell Science Publications.

Bekoff, M. (2000). Social play behavior: Cooperation, fairness, trust, and the evolution of morality. *Journal of Consciousness Studies, 8,* 81–90.

Bekoff, M., & Byers, J. (1981). A critical reanalysis of the ontogeny and phylogeny of mammalian social and locomotor play: An ethological hornet's nest. In K. Immelman, G. Barlow, I. Petrinivich, & M. Main (Eds.), *Behavioral development* (pp. 296–337). Cambridge: Cambridge University Press.

Berglund, A., & Rosenqvist, G. (2001). Male pipefish prefer dominant over attractive females. *Behavioral Ecology, 12,* 402–406.

Bergstrom, C. T., & Lachmann, M. (2003). The Red King effect: When the slowest runner wins the coevolutionary race. *Proceedings of the National Academy of Sciences, U.S.A., 100,* 593–598.

Birkhead, T. R. (1998). Cryptic female choice: Criteria for establishing female sperm choice. *Evolution, 52,* 1212–1218.

Birkhead, T. R., & Pizzari, T. (2002). Postcopulatory sexual selection. *Nature Reviews Genetics, 3,* 262–273.

Brick, O., & Jakobsson, S. (2002). Individual variation in risk taking: The effect of a predatory threat on fighting behavior in *Nannacara anomala*. *Behavioral Ecology, 13,* 439–442.

Brown, K. M. (1998). Proximate and ultimate causes of adoption in ring-billed gulls. *Animal Behaviour, 56,* 1529–1543.

Bshary, R. (2002). Biting cleaner fish use altruism to deceive image-scoring client reef fish. *Proceedings of the Royal Society of London, Series B, 269,* 2087–2093.

Bshary, R., & Grutter, A. S. (2002). Asymmetric cheating opportunities and partner control in a cleaner fish mutualism. *Animal Behaviour, 63,* 547–555.

Bshary, R., & Schaffer, D. (2002). Choosy reef fish select cleaner fish that provide high-quality service. *Animal Behaviour, 63,* 557–564.

Buckland-Nicks, J. (1998). Prosobranch parasperm: Sterile germ cells that promote paternity? *Micron, 29,* 267–280.

Bugnyar, T., & Kotrschal, K. (2002). Observational learning and the raiding of food caches in ravens, *Corvus corax:* Is it "tactical" deception? *Animal Behaviour, 64,* 185–195.

Bukacinski, D., Bukacinska, M., & Lubjuhn, T. (2000). Adoption of chicks and the level of relatedness in common gull, *Larus canus,* colonies: DNA fingerprinting analyses. *Animal Behaviour, 59,* 289–299.

Burghardt, G. M., Ward, B., & Rosscoe, R. (1996). Problem of reptile play: Environmental enrichment and play behavior in a captive Nile soft-shelled turtle, *Trionyx triunguis. Zoo Biology, 15,* 223–238.

Carlier, P., & Lefebvre, L. (1996). Differences in individual learning between group-foraging and territorial Zenaida doves. *Behaviour, 133,* 1197–1207.

Caro, T. M. (1998). *Behavioral ecology and conservation biology.* New York: Oxford University Press.

Charnov, E. L. (1973). *Optimal foraging: Some theoretical explorations.* Seattle: University of Washington Press.

Charnov, E. L. (1976). Optimal foraging, the marginal value theorem. *Theoretical Population Biology, 9,* 129–136.

Charnov, E. L., & Parker, G. A. (1995). Dimensionless invariants from foraging theory's marginal value theorem. *Proceedings of the National Academy of Sciences, U.S.A., 92,* 1446–1450.

Clark, A. M. (1996). Natural products as a resource for new drugs. *Pharmaceutical Research, 12,* 1133–1141.

Clutton-Brock, T. H. (1998). Reproductive skew, concessions and limited control. *Trends in Ecology and Evolution, 13,* 288–292.

Clutton-Brock, T. H., Brotherton, P. N. M., Russell, A. F., O'Riain, M. J., Gaynor, D., Kansky, R., Griffin, A., Manser, M., Sharpe, L., McIlrath, G. M., Small, T., Moss, A., & Monfort, S. (2001). Cooperation, control and concession in meerkat groups. *Science, 291,* 478–491.

Collins, E. J., Houston, A. I., & Lang, A. (2002). The ideal free distribution: An analysis of the perceptual limit model. *Evolutionary Ecology Research, 4,* 471–493.

Cook, J. M., Bean, D., & Power, S. (1999). Fatal fighting in fig wasps—GBH in time and space. *Trends in Ecology and Evolution, 14,* 257–259.

Cowan, M. M. (1999). Plant products as antimicrobial agents. *Clinical Microbiology Reviews, 12,* 564–582.

Cowlishaw, G. (1997). Trade-offs between foraging and predation risk determine habitat use in a desert baboon population. *Animal Behaviour, 53,* 667–686.

Crespi, B. J. (2000). The evolution of maladaptation. *Heredity, 84*, 623–629.

Curtsinger, J. W., Service, P. M., & Prout, T. (1994). Antagonistic pleiotropy, reversal of dominance, and genetic-polymorphism. *American Naturalist, 144*, 210–228.

Cushing, B. S., & Reese, E. (1999). Hawk-like aggression in the Hawaiian red lobster, *Enoplometopus occidentalis. Behaviour, 135*, 863–877.

Daly, M., & Wilson, M. (1988). *Homicide.* New York: Aldine de Gruyter.

Daly, M., & Wilson, M. (1996). Violence against stepchildren. *Current Directions in Psychological Science, 5*, 77–81.

Darwin, C. (1859). *On the origin of species.* London: J. Murray.

Dawkins, R., & Krebs, J. R. (1978). Animal signals: Information for manipulation? In J. R. Krebs & N. B. Davies (Eds.), *Behavioural ecology* (pp. 282–315). Sunderland, MA: Sinauer Associates.

Debat, V., & David, P. (2001). Mapping phenotypes: Canalization, plasticity and developmental stability. *Trends in Ecology and Evolution, 16*, 555–561.

Dell'Oro, G. (2002). *Behavioral ecotoxicology.* New York: Wiley.

Descrochers, A., Belisle, M., & Bourque, J. (2002). Do mobbing calls affect the perception of predation risk by forest birds? *Animal Behaviour, 64*, 709–714.

DeSmet, P. A. G. M. (1997). The role of plant-derived drugs and herbal medicines in healthcare. *Drugs, 54*, 801–840.

Domjan, M., & Hollis, K. L. (1988). Reproductive behavior: A potential model system for adaptive specializations in learning. In R. C. Bolles & M. D. Beecher (Eds.), *Evolution and learning* (pp. 213–237). Hillsdale, NJ: Lawrence Erlbaum Associates.

Dugatkin, L. A. (1992). Sexual selection and imitation: Females copy the mate choice of others. *American Naturalist, 139*, 1384–1389.

Dugatkin, L. A. (2002). Animal cooperation among unrelated individuals. *Naturwissenschaften, 89*, 533–541.

Eason, P. K., & Stamps, J. A. (1992). The effect of visibility on territory size and shape. *Behavioral Ecology, 3*, 166–172.

Eberhard, W. G. (2000). Criteria for demonstrating postcopulatory female choice. *Evolution, 54*, 1047–1050.

Eklund, A. (1996). The effects of inbreeding on aggression in wild male house mice (*Mus domesticus*). *Behaviour, 133*, 883–901.

Emlen, S. T. (1995). An evolutionary theory of the family. *Proceedings of the National Academy of Sciences, U.S.A., 92*, 8092–8099.

Endler, J. A. (1992). Signals, signal conditions, and the direction of evolution. *American Naturalist, Supplement, 139*, S125–S153.

Enquist, M., & Leimar, O. (1990). The evolution of fatal fighting. *Animal Behaviour, 39*, 1–9.

Evans, J. P., Kelley, J. L., Ramnarine, I. W., & Pilastro, A. (2002). Female behaviour mediates male courtship under predation risk in the guppy (*Poecilia reticulata*). *Behavioral Ecology and Sociobiology, 52,* 496–502.

Ewald, P. W. (1993). The evolution of virulence. *Scientific American,* April issue, pp. 86–93.

Ewald, P. W. (2000). *Plague time.* New York: The Free Press.

Forsgren, E., Kvarnemo, C., & Lindstrom, K. (1996). Mode of sexual selection determined by resource abundance in two sand goby populations. *Evolution, 50,* 646–654.

Fraser, S. A., Wisenden, B. D., & Keenleyside, M. H. A. (1993). Aggressive behavior among convict cichlid (*Cichlasoma nigrofasciatum*) fry of different sizes and its importance to brood adoption. *Canadian Journal of Zoology, 71,* 2358–2362.

Galvani, A. P. (2003). Epidemiology meets evolutionary ecology. *Trends in Ecology and Evolution, 18,* 132–139.

Gibert, P., Moreteau, B., Moreteau, J.-C., & David, J. R. (1998). Genetic variability of quantitative traits in *Drosophila melanogaster* (fruit fly) natural populations: Analysis of wild-living flies and of several laboratory generations. *Heredity, 80,* 326–335.

Grammer, K., & Thornhill, R. (1994). Human (*Homo sapiens*) facial attractiveness and sexual selection—the role of symmetry and averageness. *Journal of Comparative Psychology, 108,* 233–242.

Griffiths, P. E. (1996). The historical turn in the study of adaptation. *British Journal for the Philosophy of Science, 47,* 511–532.

Gross, M. R. (2002). All together now: Large numbers of bacteria can coordinate their activities by a form of chemical communication known as quorum sensing. *Chemistry in Britain, 38,* 22.

Gross, M. R. (1996). Alternative reproductive strategies and tactics: Diversity within sexes. *Trends in Ecology and Evolution, 11,* 92–98.

Gould, S. J., & Lewontin, R. (1979). The spandrels of San Marcos and the Panglossian paradigm: A critique of the adaptationist programme. *Proceedings of the Royal Society of London, 205,* 581–598.

Healey, S., & Krebs, J. R. (1992). Food storing and the hippocampus in corvids: Amount and volume are correlated. *Proceedings of the Royal Society of London, 248,* 241–245.

Hedrick, P. W. (1999). Antagonistic pleiotropy and genetic polymorphism: A perspective. *Heredity, 82,* 126–133.

Hoffmann, A. A. (1999). Is the heritability for courtship and mating speed in *Drosophila* (fruit fly) low? *Heredity, 82,* 158–162.

Hsu, Y., & Wolf, L. L. (1999). The winner and loser effects: Integrating multiple experiences. *Animal Behaviour, 57,* 903–910.

Jenni, D., & Collier, G. (1972). Polyandry in the American jacana (*Jacana spinosa*). *Auk, 89,* 743–765.

Jerison, H. (1970). Brain evolution: New light on old principles. *Science, 170,* 1224–1225.

Jivoff, P. (1997). The relative roles of predation and sperm competition on the duration of the post-copulatory association between the sexes in the blue crab, *Callinectes sapidus. Behavioral Ecology and Sociobiology, 40,* 175–185.

Johnstone, R. A. (1998). Conspiratorial whispers and conspicuous displays: Games of signal detection. *Evolution, 52,* 1554–1563.

Karamura, S. (1959). The process of sub-culture propagation among Japanese macaques. *Primates, 2,* 43–60.

Keller, L. F., Grant, P. R., Grant, B. R., & Petren, K. (2001). Heritability of morphological traits in Darwin's finches: Misidentified paternity and maternal effects. *Heredity, 87,* 325–336.

Kempenaers, B., Foerster, K., Questiau, S., Robertson, B. C.. & Vermeirssen, E. L. M. (2000). Distinguishing between female sperm choice versus male sperm competition: A comment on Birkhead. *Evolution, 54,* 1050–1052.

Kirkpatrick, M., & Ryan, M. (1991). The evolution of mating preferences and the paradox of the lek. *Nature, 350,* 33–38.

Koolhaas, J. M., Korte, S. M., De Boer, S. F., Van Der Vegt, B. J., Van Reenen, C. G., Hopster, H., De Jong, I. C., Ruis, M. A. W., & Blokhuis, H. J. (1999). Coping styles in animals: Current status in behavior and stress-physiology. *Neuroscience and Biobehavioral Reviews, 23,* 925–935.

Koops, M. A., & Abrahams, M. V. (1999). Assessing the ideal free distribution: Do guppies use aggression as public information about patch quality? *Ethology, 105,* 737–746.

Koops, M. A., & Abrahams, M. V. (2003). Integrating the roles of information and competitive ability on the spatial distribution of social foragers. *American Naturalist, 161,* 586–600.

Krams, I., & Krama, T. (2002). Interspecific reciprocity explains mobbing behaviour of the breeding chaffinches, *Fringilla coelebs. Proceedings of the Royal Society of London, Series B, 269,* 2345–2350.

Krause, M. A., Burghardt, G. M., & Lentini, A. (1999). Object provisioning for Nile soft-shelled turtles (*Trionyx triunguis*). *Lab Animal, 28,* 38–41.

Kruuk, L. E. B., Slate, J., Pemberton, J. M., Brotherstone, S., Guinness, F., & Clutton-Brock, T. (2002). Antler size in red deer: Heritability and selection but no evolution. *Evolution, 56,* 1683–1695.

Laland, K. N., & Williams, K. (1998). Social transmission of maladaptive information in the guppy. *Behavioral Ecology, 9,* 493–499.

Leimar, O. (1997). Reciprocity and communication of partner quality. *Proceedings of the Royal Society of London, Series B, 264,* 1209–1215.

Lima, S. L. (1995). Back to the basics of anti-predator vigilance: The group-size effect. *Animal Behaviour, 49*, 11–20.

Marriner, L. M., & Drickamer, L. C. (1994). Factors influencing stereotyped behavior of primates in a zoo. *Zoo Biology, 13*, 267–275.

Maynard Smith, J. (1976). Evolution and the theory of games. *American Scientist, 64*, 41–45.

Maynard Smith, J. (1982). *Evolution and the theory of games.* Cambridge: Cambridge University Press.

McChesney, J. D. (1993). Biological and chemical diversity and the search for new pharmaceuticals and other bioactive natural products. *ACS Symposium Series, 534*, 38–47.

McEwen, B. S., & Wingfield, J. C. (2003). The concept of allostasis in biology and biomedicine. *Hormones and Behavior, 43*, 2–15.

McGinn, K. L., Thompson, L., & Bazerman, M. H. (2003). Dyadic processes of disclosure and reciprocity in bargaining with communication. *Journal of Behavioral Decision Making, 16*, 17–34.

McGregor, P. K., & Peake, T. M. (2000). Communication networks: Social environments for receiving and signalling. *Acta Ethologica, 2*, 71–81.

Meagher, S., Penn, D. J., & Potts, W. K. (2000). Male-male competition magnifies inbreeding depression in wild house mice. *Proceedings of the National Academy of Sciences, U.S.A., 97*, 3324–3329.

Mellen, J., & MacPhee, M. S. (2001). Philosophy of environmental enrichment: Past, present, and future. *Zoo Biology, 20*, 211–226.

Milinski, M., Semmann, D., Bakker, T. C. M., & Krambeck, H.-J. (2001). Cooperation through indirect reciprocity: Image scoring or standing strategy? *Proceedings of the Royal Society of London, Series B, 268*, 2495–2501.

Milinski, M., & Wedekind, C. (1998). Working memory constrains human cooperation in the Prisoner's Dilemma. *Proceedings of the National Academy of Sciences, U.S.A., 95*, 13755–13758.

Miller, G. T., & Pitnick, S. (2002). Sperm-female coevolution in *Drosophila*. *Science, 298*, 1230–1233.

Miller, M. B., & Bassler, B. L. (2001). Quorum sensing in bacteria. *Annual Reviews of Microbiology, 55*, 165–199.

Mirza, R. S., Scott, J. J., & Chivers, D. P. (2001). Differential responses of male and female red swordtails to chemical alarm cues. *Journal of Fish Biology, 59*, 716–728.

Moczek, A. P., & Emlen, D. J. (2000). Male horn dimorphism in the scarab beetle, *Onthophagus taurus*: Do alternative reproductive tactics favor alternative phenotypes? *Animal Behaviour, 59*, 459–466.

Møller, A. P., & Erritzøe, J. (1998). Host immune defence and migration in birds. *Evolutionary Ecology, 12*, 945–953.

Naguib, M. (2003). Reverberation of rapid and slow trills: Implications for signal adaptations to long-range communication. *Journal of the Acoustical Society of America, 113,* 1749–1756.

Naguib, M., Mundry, R., Ostreiher, R., Hultsch, H., Schrader, L., & Todt, D. (1999). Cooperatively breeding Arabian babblers call differently when mobbing in different predator-induced situations. *Behavioral Ecology, 10,* 636–640.

Neat, F. C., Taylor, A. C., & Huntingford, F. A. (1998). Proximate costs of fighting in male cichlid fish: The role of injuries and energy metabolism. *Animal Behaviour, 55,* 875–882.

Nilsson, S. O., & Nilsson, G. E. (2000). Free choice by female sticklebacks: Lack of preference for male dominance traits. *Canadian Journal of Zoology, 78,* 1251–1258.

Novak, M. A. (2003). Self-injurious behavior in rhesus monkeys: New insights into its etiology, physiology, and treatment. *American Journal of Primatology, 59,* 3–19.

Nowak, M., & Sigmund, K. (1993). A strategy of win-stay, lose-shift that outperforms tit-for-tat in the Prisoner's Dilemma game. *Nature, 364,* 56–58.

Ord, T. J., Blumstein, D. T., & Evans, C. S. (2002). Ecology and signal evolution in lizards. *Biological Journal of the Linnean Society, 77,* 127–148.

Pandy, R. C. (1998). Prospecting for potentially new pharmaceuticals from natural sources. *Medicinal Research Reviews, 18,* 333–346.

Parker, G. A., & Simmons, L. W. (1994). Evolution of phenotypic optima and copula duration in dungflies. *Nature, 370,* 53–56.

Parker, G. A., Simmons, L. W., Stockley, P., McChristie, D. M., & Charnov, E. L. (1999). Optimal copula duration in yellow dungflies: Effects of female size and egg content. *Animal Behaviour, 57,* 795–805.

Parker, G. A., Simmons, L. W., & Ward, P. I. (1993). Optimal copula duration in dungflies: Effects of frequency dependence and female mating status. *Behavioral Ecology and Sociobiology, 32,* 157–166.

Parker, G. A., & Stuart, R. A. (1976). Animal behavior as a strategy optimizer: Evolution of resource assessment strategies and optimal emigration thresholds. *American Naturalist, 110,* 1055–1076.

Pellis, S., & Iwaniuk, A. (1999). The roles of phylogeny and sociality in the evolution of social play in muriod rodents. *Animal Behaviour, 58,* 361–373.

Phelan, J. P., Archer, M. A., Beckman, K. A., Chippindale, A. K., Nusbaum, T. J., & Rose, M. R. (2003). Breakdown in correlations during laboratory evolution. I. Comparative analyses of *Drosophila* populations. *Evolution, 57,* 527–535.

Pitnick, S., & Brown, W. D. (2000). Criteria for demonstrating female sperm choice. *Evolution, 54,* 1052–1056.

Pitnick, S., Spicer, G. S., & Markow, T. A. (1995). How long is a giant sperm? *Nature, 375,* 109.

Popper, A. N. (1996). The teleost octavolateralis system: Structure and function. *Marine and Freshwater Behavior and Physiology, 27,* 95–100.

Powell, S. B., Newman, H. A., McDonald, T. A., Bugenhagen, P., & Lewis, M. H. (2000). Development of spontaneous stereotyped behavior in deer mice: Effects of early and late exposure to a more complex environment. *Developmental Psychobiology, 37,* 100–108.

Powell, S. B., Newman, H. A., Pendergast, J. F., & Lewis, M. H. (1999). A rodent model of spontaneous stereotypy: Initial characterization of developmental, environmental, and neurobiological factors. *Physiology and Behavior, 66,* 355–363.

Price, E. O. (2003). *Animal domestication and behavior.* New York: CABI Publishing.

Pulliam, R. (1973). On the advantages of flocking. *Journal of Theoretical Biology, 38,* 419–422.

Qvarnstrom, A., & Forsgren, E. (1998). Should females prefer dominant males? *Trends in Ecology and Evolution, 13,* 498–501.

Radinsky, L. (1978). Evolution of brain size in carnivores and ungulates. *American Naturalist, 112,* 815–831.

Reavis, R. H., & Grober, M. S. (1999). An integrative approach to sex change: Social, behavioural and neurochemical changes in *Lythrypnus dalli* (Pisces). *Acta Ethologica, 2,* 51–60.

Ramcharan, E. J., Gnadt, J. W., & Sherman, S. M. (2003). Single-unit recording in the lateral geniculate nucleus of the awake behaving monkey. *Methods, 30,* 142–151.

Reeve, H. K., & Sherman, P. W. (1993). Adaptation and the goals of evolutionary research. *Quarterly Review of Biology, 68,* 1–32.

Rendell, L., & Whitehead, H. (2001). Culture in whales and dolphins. *Brain and Behavioral Sciences, 24,* 309–324.

Riesecker, J., Skelly, D. K., Beard, K., & Preisser, E. (1999). Behavioral reduction of infectious risk. *Proceedings of the National Academy of Sciences, U.S.A., 96,* 9165–9168.

Roberts, G. (1996). Why individual vigilance declines as group size increases. *Animal Behaviour, 51,* 1077–1086.

Robinson, J. V., & Novak, K. L. (1997). The relationship between mating system and penis morphology in ishnuran damselflies (Odonata: Coenagrionidae). *Biological Journal of the Linnean Society, 60,* 187–200.

Roozendaal, B. (2002). Stress and memory: Opposing effects of glucocorticoids on memory consolidation and memory retrieval. *Neurobiology of Learning and Memory, 78,* 578–595.

Rose, M. R., & Mueller, L. D. (1998). Evolution of human lifespan: Past, future, and present. *American Journal of Human Biology, 10*, 409–420.

Ryan, B. C., & Vandenbergh, J. G. (2002). Intrauterine position effects. *Neuroscience and Biobehavioral Reviews, 26*, 665–678.

Ryan, M. J. (1997). Sexual selection and mate choice. In J. R. Krebs & N. B. Davies (Eds.), *Behavioural ecology: An evolutionary approach*, 4th ed. Oxford: Blackwell Scientific Publications.

Ryan, M. J., & Rosenthal, G. G. (2001). Variation and selection in swordtails. In L. A. Dugatkin (Ed.), *Model systems in behavioral ecology* (pp. 133–148). Princeton: Princeton University Press.

Sally, D. F. (1995). Conversation and cooperation in social dilemmas: Experimental evidence from 1958 to 1992. *Rationality and Society, 7*, 58–92.

Schuett, G. W., Clark, D. L., & Kraus, F. (1984). Feeding mimicry in the rattlesnake *Sistrurus catenatus*, with comment on the evolution of the rattle. *Animal Behaviour, 32*, 625–626.

Schuett, G. W., & Grober, M. S. (2000). Post-fight levels of plasma lactate and corticosterone in male copperheads, *Agkistrodon contortrix* (Serpentes, Viperidae): Differences between winners and losers. *Physiology and Behavior, 71*, 335–341.

Sherman, P. W., Reeve, H. K., & Pfennig, D. W. (1997). Recognition systems. In J. R. Krebs & N. B. Davies (Eds.), *Behavioural ecology: An evolutionary approach*, 4th ed. (pp. 69–96). Oxford: Blackwell Scientific Publications.

Shors, T. J. (2001). Acute stress rapidly and persistently enhances memory formation in the male rat. *Neurobiology of Learning and Memory, 75*, 10–29.

Sih, A., Lauer, M., & Krupa, J. J. (2002). Path analysis and the relative importance of male-female conflict, female choice and male-male competition in water striders. *Animal Behaviour, 63*, 1079–1089.

Spinka, M., Newberry, R., & Bekoff, M. (2001). Mammalian play: Training for the unexpected. *Quarterly Review of Biology, 76*, 141–168.

Stamps, J. A., & Krishnan, V. V. (2001). How territorial animals compete for divisible space: A learning-based model with unequal competitors. *American Naturalist, 157*, 154–169.

Strassman, J. E., Solis, C. R., Hughes, C. R., Goodnight, K. F., & Queller, D. C. (1997). Colony life history and demography of a swarm-founding social wasp. *Behavioral Ecology and Sociobiology, 40*, 71–77.

Swaddle, J. P., & Cuthill, I. C. (1995). Asymmetry and human facial attractiveness—symmetry may not always be beautiful. *Proceedings of the Royal Society of London, Series B, 261*, 111–116.

Taborsky, M. (1994). Sneakers, satellites, and helpers: Parasite and cooperative behavior in fish reproduction. *Advances in the Study of Behavior, 23*, 1–97.

Tanner, J. E. (2001). The influence of clonality on demography: Patterns in expected longevity and survivorship. *Ecology, 82*, 1971–1981.

Tebbich, S., Bshary, R., & Grutter, A. S. (2002). Cleaner fish *Labroides dimidiatus* recognise familiar clients. *Animal Cognition, 5*, 139–145.

Tiefenbacher, S., Novak, M. A., Jorgensen, M. J., & Meyer, J. S. (2000). Physiological correlates of self-injurious behavior in captive, socially-reared rhesus monkeys. *Psychoneuroendocrinology, 25*, 799–817.

Tooby, J., & Cosmides, L. (1989). Evolutionary psychology and the generation of culture, Part I. *Ethology and Sociobiology, 10*, 29–49.

Van Schaik, C. P., Ancrenaz, M., Borgen, G., Galdikas, B., Knott, C. D., Singleton, I., Suzuki, A., Utami, S. S., & Merrill, M. (2003). Orangutan cultures and the evolution of material culture. *Science, 299*, 102–105.

Van Valen, L. (1973). A new evolutionary law. *Evolutionary Theory, 1*, 1–31.

Warner, R. R., Robertson, D. R., & Leigh, E. G. (1975). Sex change and sexual selection. *Science, 190*, 633–638.

Wedekind, C., & Milinski, M. (1996). Human cooperation in the simultaneous and the alternating Prisoner's dilemma: Pavlov versus generous tit-for-tat. *Proceedings of the National Academy of Science, U.S.A., 93*, 2686–2689.

Wedekind, C., & Milinski, M. (2000). Cooperation through image scoring in humans. *Science, 288*, 850–852.

Weir, A. A. S., Chappell, J., & Kacelnik, A. (2002). Shaping of hooks in new Caledonian crows. *Science, 297*, 981.

West, S. A., Murray, M. G., Machado, C. A., Griffin, A. S., & Herre, E. A. (2001). Testing Hamilton's rule with competition between relatives. *Nature, 409*, 510–513.

Whitehead, N. A., Barnard, A. M. L., Slater, H., Simpson, N. J. L., & Salmond, G. P. C. (2001). Quorum-sensing in Gram-negative bacteria. *FEMS Microbiology Reviews, 25*, 365–404.

Wilkinson, G. (1984). Reciprocal food sharing in vampire bats. *Nature, 308*, 181–184.

Williams, G. C. (1957). Pleiotropy, natural selection, and the evolution of senescence. *Evolution, 11*, 398–411.

Wingfield, J. C., Maney, D. L., Breuner, C. W., Jacobs, J. D., Lynn, S., Ramenofsky, M., & Richardson, R. D. (1998). Ecological bases of hormone-behavior interactions: The "emergency life history stage." *American Zoologist, 38*, 191–206.

Wisenden, B. D. (1999). Alloparental care in fishes. *Reviews in Fish Biology and Fisheries, 9*, 45–70.

Wisenden, B. D., & Keenleyside, M. H. A. (1992). Intraspecific brood adoption in convict cichlids—a mutual benefit. *Behavioral Ecology and Sociobiology, 31*, 263–269.

Wisenden, B. D., & Keenleyside, M. H. A. (1994). The dilution effect and differential predation following brood adoption in free-ranging convict cichlids (*Cichlasoma nigrofasciatum*). *Ethology, 96*, 203–212.

Withers, H., Swift, S., & Williams, P. (2001). Quorum sensing as an integral component of gene regulatory networks in Gram-negative bacteria. *Current Opinion in Microbiology, 4*, 186–193.

Wright, J., Berg, E., de Kort, S. R., Khazin, V., & Maklakov, A. A. (2001). Safe selfish sentinels in a cooperative bird. *Journal of Animal Ecology, 70*, 1070–1079.